T0316251

ANNE Oꜰ GREEN GABLES

L M Montgomery
ANNE OF GREEN GABLES
Adapted by
Emma Reeves

OBERON BOOKS
LONDON

First published in 2004 by Oberon Books Ltd

521 Caledonian Road, London N7 9RH

Tel: +44 (0) 20 7607 3637 / Fax: +44 (0) 20 7607 3629

e-mail: info@oberonbooks.com

www.oberonbooks.com

A catalogue record for this book is available from the British Library.

PB ISBN: 9781840025385

E ISBN: 9781783192472

Cover image by Kean | Lanyon www.keanlanyon.com

Converted by Replika Press PVT Ltd., India

Visit www.oberonbooks.com to read more about all our books and to buy them. You will also find features, author interviews and news of any author events, and you can sign up for e-newsletters so that you're always first to hear about our new releases.

Characters

KATIE MAURICE

JOSIE PYE

RUBY GILLIS

MARIAN

MR CARR

MRS RACHEL LYNDE

MRS BARRY

DIANA BARRY

MARILLA CUTHBERT

ANNE SHIRLEY

MATTHEW CUTHBERT

MRS BLEWETT

GILBERT BLYTHE

MISS STACY

MISS HARRIS

Setting

A British school classroom. Wooden chairs, desks,
a table for the teacher. A blackboard.
Elsewhere on stage is Green Gables, in the village of Avonlea.
The action takes place continuously, with changes of location
indicated by lighting.

This version of *Anne of Green Gables* was first performed at the Lilian Baylis Theatre, Sadler's Wells, on 25 November 2004, with the following cast:

KATIE MAURICE, Kali Nicholson

JOSIE PYE / MRS BLEWETT, Beccy Armory

RUBY GILLIS / MRS BARRY, Joanna Croll

MARILLA CUTHBERT / MARIAN, Jenny Lee

MATTHEW CUTHBERT / MR CARR, David Baron

MRS LYNDE / MISS STACY, Tina Gray

DIANA BARRY, Lisa Hewitt

ANNE SHIRLEY, Ruth Gibson

GILBERT BLYTHE, Matt Canavan

Understudies, Laura Stevely and Jessica Woolf

Other parts played by members of the company.

Adapted by Emma Reeves

Directed by Andrew Loudon

Designed by Rachel Payne

Lighting by Matthew Eagland

Music by Paul Weir

Singing supervisor, Sue Appleby

Produced by Mark Bentley

Company Stage Manager, Lindah Balfour

Deputy Stage Manager, Jo Oliver

Wardrobe and Wig Mistress, Laura Smith

Wardrobe Supervision, Lesley Huckstepp

Wig Supervision, Louise Ricci

ACT I

As the audience enter, KATIE, a young girl of 13 or so, is absorbed in a copy of Anne of Green Gables. *Her clothes are old-fashioned and shabby, but contemporary, not 1880s. She has an old school bag with her – it's very battered; like KATIE and her clothes, it has seen better days.*

MODERN JOSIE AND RUBY enter and immediately target KATIE.

JOSIE: Hey, pikey! Minger! Hippy! You smelly little freak, I'm talking to you.

KATIE ignores her.

What's the matter, no speaka de English?

KATIE still ignores her. JOSIE crosses and snaps her fingers in front of KATIE's face.

Hel – *lo?*

KATIE: I am only reading –

JOSIE: Time to go home now, innit? Oh yeah – you haven't got one.

KATIE: Excuse me, please.

KATIE tries to move but JOSIE blocks her way.

JOSIE: I saw you lookin' at me in class. Givin' me the evils.

KATIE: I did not know I should not look.

KATIE tries to push past but JOSIE grabs her by the hair. KATIE cries out in pain.

JOSIE: You wanna know something funny? My taxes pay for you.

KATIE: What taxes?

JOSIE: (*Ignoring her.*) That means I own you, yeah? Yeah?

RUBY: Cleaner's coming.

JOSIE: Do I look like I give one?

But she releases KATIE.

(*Threatening.*) See you on the way home, scrounger.

MARIAN, a harassed woman in late middle age wearing a cleaner's overalls, watches disapprovingly as JOSIE and RUBY slope off.

MARIAN: Mr Carr's about to lock up. You should be getting off home, young lady.

KATIE: I do not think so, no.

She goes back to her book.

MARIAN: Hasn't your mother ever told you it's rude to answer back?

KATIE: I do not understand.

MARIAN: Right. That's it. (*Calls.*) Mr Carr!

MR CARR, the head caretaker, enters. He is a calm, gentle character in his 60s.

MR CARR: What's the problem, ladies?

MARIAN: Cheeky little cow won't move off school property, I've got my job to do, can't be hanging around waiting after hooligans – don't know they're born, this lot.

KATIE: (*Simultaneously.*) I have done nothing, she just came and shouted at me – I was only reading, is it a crime to read here?

MR CARR: Hey – Hey! Bit of hush please!

They shut up.

What you reading there, lass?

KATIE: A book.

MARIAN: Don't you talk to Mr Carr like that! (*To MR CARR.*) You see? This is what happens when we let this lot in our schools.

MR CARR: You just get on, now. I'll deal with this.

MARIAN goes, muttering.

MARIAN: Think they can do what they like. We shouldn't have to put up with it.

KATIE is braced for a confrontation, but MR CARR is relaxed.

MR CARR: I don't have to lock up just yet. Let's give it half an hour or so. Let them lasses get bored and go home, eh?

KATIE: All right.

KATIE sits down, wary. MR CARR looks at her book.

MR CARR: *Anne of Green Gables.* That's an American story, in't it?

KATIE: Canadian.

MR CARR: I never was any good with the geography. Couldn't get interested in all them foreign parts. Too far away.

KATIE: I like far-away places.

MR CARR: Do you now?

KATIE: Anywhere that is not here.

MR CARR: (*Calm.*) So, tell us about Canada, then.

KATIE: I only know this book.

MR CARR: Then let's hear about that.

KATIE: Well... the story happens in the village of Avonlea, on Prince Edward Island.

MR CARR: Go on.

KATIE: (*Reads.*) Avonlea occupied a little triangular peninsula jutting out into the Gulf of St Lawrence. So anybody who went in or out had to pass over the hill road, and run the gauntlet of Mrs Rachel Lynde's all-seeing eye.

Cross-fade. Lighting change to indicate a June day. The sound of bees, and music, as we move into the story world.

She would sit for hours at her window, keeping a sharp eye on the main road that crossed the hollow and wound up the steep red hill beyond...

Mrs Lynde's House

MRS LYNDE, a gossip with a heart of gold, is taking tea with her neighbour, the superior MRS BARRY, and bored teenager DIANA BARRY. All wear fashionable 1880s clothes.

MRS LYNDE: Well, I never! Mrs Barry, Diana, what do you make of *that?*

DIANA and MRS BARRY follow her gesture and look out of the window.

MRS BARRY: I don't see, Rachel –

MRS LYNDE: There!

DIANA: That's only old Mr Cuthbert.

MRS LYNDE: (*Triumphant.*) Matthew Cuthbert! Driving by at half-past three in the afternoon – when he's supposed to be planting turnips!

MRS BARRY: Maybe he's run out of seed?

MRS LYNDE: Then why would he be wearing his best collar?

MRS BARRY: I daresay he's visiting up town.

MRS LYNDE: He *never* visits.

DIANA: Perhaps he's going for the doctor?

MRS LYNDE: No, child, he wasn't driving nearly fast enough. Well, I'm clean puzzled, that's what.

MRS BARRY: Oh, for mercy's sake, Rachel. Why don't you just go over to Green Gables and ask Marilla?

MRS LYNDE: I'm never one to interfere in my neighbours' business, Mrs Barry. (*Pause.*) But, now you put me in mind of Marilla, she had a quilting-frame from me last winter and never got round to returning it. Likely she's finished with it now – I'll just – step over to Green Gables.

MRS BARRY: (*Simultaneously.*) – step over to Green Gables.

MRS LYNDE: And I expect you'll be walking home by the main road?

MRS BARRY: No, I – I think this once we'll cut through the woods.

MRS LYNDE: Past Green Gables?

MRS BARRY: (*Reluctantly.*) Past Green Gables.

They leave together, followed by DIANA. Music.

Green Gables – Kitchen

MARILLA CUTHBERT enters. She is a stern woman in her 60s, dressed in simple, plain, 1880s clothes.

MARILLA: Good afternoon Rachel – Mrs Barry – Diana. And how are all your folks?

MRS BARRY: We're all pretty well.

MRS LYNDE: We were kind of afraid *you* weren't, though, when we saw Matthew drive off today. Thought maybe he was going for the doctor?

MARILLA: Oh no – we're both quite well. Although –

The other women lean forward, alert for gossip.

– I had a bad headache yesterday.

DIANA: Miss Cuthbert, we're awful keen to know – Where has Mr Cuthbert gone today?

MARILLA: Matthew's gone to meet the train at Bright River. We're adopting a child from an orphan asylum in Nova Scotia.

They take in the momentous news.

MRS LYNDE: What on *earth* put such a notion into your head?

MARILLA: You know we're not so spry as we once were. Matthew's heart troubles him a great deal – he needs help with the farm. We heard that Mrs Spencer was off to the Hopetown Asylum to get a little girl, so we sent her word to pick us up a smart, likely boy of fourteen or so.

MRS LYNDE: That's just your Diana's age, ain't it?

MRS BARRY: What of that? She won't have anything to do with him.

DIANA: Mother! He'd be living so near – he could be a friend –

MRS BARRY: What do you want friends for? You've got your sister.

DIANA: Minnie May's a *baby*!

MRS BARRY: Diana, you are not to associate with some asylum boy from goodness knows where! No offence, Marilla. If it was a girl, now –

MARILLA: I'm not getting a girl!

MRS LYNDE: You're still doing a mighty foolish thing. Didn't you hear about that case up West? A man and his wife took a boy from an orphan asylum, and do you know what he did?

MARILLA: We soon will.

MRS LYNDE: Set fire to the house *on purpose* and burnt them all in their beds! And you mind that foundling boy up at Carmody? Used to suck eggs. They couldn't break him of it.

MRS BARRY: It's a terrible risky thing you're doing, Marilla.

MARILLA: So is pretty much everything in this world. There's a risk in having children of your own – they don't always turn out well.

MRS BARRY: The *Barry* children do.

MRS LYNDE: Well, don't say I didn't warn you if he poisons the water.

MARILLA: *What?*

MRS LYNDE: An orphan in New Brunswick put strychnine in the well, and the whole family died in fearful agonies. Only it was a girl, in that instance.

MARILLA: (*Exasperated.*) I've told you Rachel, I'm not getting a girl!

Bright River Station / The Classroom

Cross-fade (as KATIE speaks) to Bright River Station.

Early evening. We see KATIE with her book, and her battered school bag. At the other side of the stage, mirroring her, sits ANNE SHIRLEY. She is young, thin, with long red braids. She wears a short, tight, 1880s-style dress of yellowish-grey and a faded brown sailor hat. She carries a battered carpet bag. Her body is tense with expectation.

KATIE: But a girl was the only creature in sight, when Matthew Cuthbert reached Bright River station.

MR CARR enters, now transformed into MATTHEW CUTHBERT. He is dressed in 1880s clothes and has a

Canadian accent. He looks up and down the platform, without seeing ANNE. Then he notices her.

Matthew dreaded all women except Marilla and Mrs Lynde. He was afraid they were secretly laughing at him. And he may have been right.

MATTHEW walks slowly towards ANNE. She looks up, quivering with expectation. MATTHEW nods nervously and walks straight past her. Once safely by, he pauses to recover from the stressful encounter.

But in Prince Edward Island, you must nod to everyone you meet, whether you know them or not.

MATTHEW looks around, puzzled. He satisfies himself that there really is nobody else about, and turns to walk back past ANNE. ANNE leaps to her feet and intercepts him. He's startled.

ANNE: Are you Mr Matthew Cuthbert of Green Gables?

MATTHEW: Well now, I suppose I am.

ANNE: Oh, I'm so glad! Can you imagine, I was beginning to be afraid you weren't coming for me!

MATTHEW: (*Confused.*) Coming for – *you?*

ANNE: I thought I might have to go back to the asylum. I don't suppose you've ever been an orphan in an asylum, but it's worse than anything you could possibly imagine. It seems so wonderful that I'm going to belong to you.

MATTHEW: Well now – seems –

ANNE: (*Interrupting.*) I've never belonged anywhere, you see. Not really…

MATTHEW: (*Desperate.*) – there's been some kind of – misunderstanding –

ANNE: What kind of misunderstanding?

MATTHEW: I got held up. Sorry I was late.

MATTHEW goes to pick up ANNE's bag.

ANNE: Oh, I'll take my bag, Mr Cuthbert. I've got all my worldly goods in it, but it isn't heavy. And if it isn't carried in a certain way the handle pulls out.

MATTHEW: Put it in the buggy, then. We've to drive a piece to Green Gables.

They walk to his buggy and sit down. MATTHEW takes the reins, and they set off.

ANNE: I've heard that Prince Edward Island is the most beautiful place in the world. Living here will make me *nearly* happy. As happy as I can be with (*Holding out her braid.*) – well, what colour would you call this?

MATTHEW: Red, ain't it?

ANNE: Yes it is. And I can't even imagine it away. It will be my lifelong sorrow. But at least it's romantic to have a lifelong sorrow. I once read about a girl who – oh, Mr Cuthbert! What is this beautiful place?

KATIE: A stretch of road completely arched over by huge wide-spreading apple trees.

MATTHEW: This is the Avenue.

ANNE: Oh *no*. It must be the – the White Way of Delight.

MATTHEW: Kind of pretty, ain't it?

ANNE: It's wonderful. The first thing I ever saw that couldn't be improved upon by imagination. (*Indicating.*) What does that tree make you think of?

MATTHEW: Well now, I dunno.

ANNE: Why, a bride – leaning out all in blossomy white, with a misty veil. I won't ever be a bride myself, of course.

MATTHEW: How do you make that out?

ANNE: Oh, no man will want a red-headed bride, except maybe a foreign missionary – they can't be too particular, can they? But I can imagine that I'm wearing a beautiful white dress, with puffed sleeves. Can't I?

MATTHEW: (*Avoiding the question, pointing.*) That's Barry's pond.

KATIE: The water was a glory of many shifting hues – crocus and rose and ethereal green.

ANNE: The Lake of Shining Waters. Yes, that's it. There's scope for the imagination in that. Oh, this is like something out of a dream. Ever since I left the orphan asylum I've kept pinching myself to see if this day was real – but I've just remembered that if it is a dream I'd better go on dreaming as long as I can, so I'd better stop pinching myself, hadn't I? I'm talking too much aren't I?

MATTHEW: Talk as much as you like.

ANNE: Really? You don't mind? At the asylum they said children should be seen and not heard. And laughed at me for using big words.

MATTHEW: Seems to me – if you have big ideas – you need big words to express 'em.

ANNE: Matthew Cuthbert, you are a kindred spirit.

Music. Lighting change – it's dusk. MARILLA enters with a candle.

Green Gables – Kitchen

MARILLA: Matthew Cuthbert, who on earth is *that?*

MATTHEW and ANNE join MARILLA.

Where's the boy?

MATTHEW: Wasn't no boy. Only her.

MARILLA: Well, this is a pretty piece of business!

ANNE: (*Devastated.*) You don't want me? You don't want me because I'm not a boy? I should have known. I should have guessed. Nobody ever *did* want me. Ever.

MARILLA: (*To MATTHEW.*) What's the child's name? (*MATTHEW doesn't know.*) You don't even know *that?*

MATTHEW: It – kinda never came up –

MARILLA: (*To ANNE.*) Who and what are you?

ANNE: Will you please call me Cordelia Fitzgerald?

MARILLA: Is that your name?

ANNE: No, but it hardly matters if you're sending me back.

MARILLA: What is your *real* name?

ANNE: Anne Shirley. Anne with an E.

MARILLA: Anne with an *E*, were there no boys at the asylum?

ANNE: An abundance of them. But Mrs Spencer said distinctly that you wanted a girl, and she supposed I would do, and I… (*To MATTHEW.*) Why didn't you just leave me at the station? If I hadn't seen the White Way of Delight and the Lake of Shining Waters it wouldn't be so hard.

MATTHEW is guilty.

MARILLA: Well, don't get yourself in a state. We're not going to turn you out of doors tonight. (*To MATTHEW.*) She'd better eat something, anyhow.

ANNE: I can't eat. I'm in the depths of despair. Can *you* eat when you're in the depths of despair?

MARILLA: I've never been in the depths of despair.

ANNE: Did you ever imagine you were?

MARILLA: No.

ANNE: Then you cannot understand what it's like. Please don't be offended, but I fear that not a morsel can pass my lips. Not even if it were a chocolate caramel. I had a chocolate caramel once, you know. It was delicious...

MARILLA: I don't have any chocolate caramels, but I've set a good tea out for you and I don't appreciate it going to waste!

MATTHEW: I guess she's tired. Best put her to bed, Marilla.

MARILLA: She can sleep in the east gable. (*To ANNE.*) Up the stairs, the small room to your left. Take this candle. We'll sort out this mess in the morning. Good night, Anne.

ANNE: How can you say it's a *good* night when you must know it's the very worst night I've ever had?

ANNE exits.

MARILLA: This is what comes of sending word instead of going ourselves. Well, that girl will have to be sent straight back to the asylum. Won't she?

MATTHEW: I suppose so...

MARILLA: You *suppose* so?

MATTHEW: She's so set on staying here –

MARILLA: That's as maybe. *We* need a boy for the farm. What good will she be to us?

MATTHEW: We might be some good to her.

MARILLA: Matthew Cuthbert, I believe that freckled witch has put a spell on you!

MATTHEW: She's a real interesting little thing – you should have heard her talk –

MARILLA: Oh, she can talk all right. It's nothing in her favour either. We don't want an orphan girl, and if we did she isn't the style I'd pick out. There's something I don't understand about her. Now, I'll go and put her candle out before she burns us all in our beds.

MATTHEW: Just as you say, Marilla.

Music.
KATIE emerges from the shadows and watches as MARILLA bustles off and MATTHEW slowly goes off in another direction.

Green Gables – Kitchen – Next morning

KATIE: It was broad daylight when Anne awoke, and tried to remember where she was. First came a delightful thrill, then a horrible remembrance. This was Green Gables. But they didn't want her, because she wasn't a boy.

Lights up – morning, bright and cheerful. MARILLA is scrubbing the floor. ANNE slopes in.

MARILLA: Well, Anne with an E, would you object if I wished you a good morning?

ANNE: Not at all. Although to me, the world is a howling wilderness, I am determined to bear up under affliction. I *am* still under affliction, aren't I?

MARILLA: I don't know what you mean by that. I do know that Matthew's driven over to Mrs Spencer, to arrange about sending you home.

ANNE: You mean back to the asylum.

MARILLA: Thank you for correcting me, yes.

MARILLA continues to scrub the floor.

ANNE: Would you like me to help you, Miss Cuthbert?

MARILLA: Can you scrub floors right?

ANNE: Pretty well. I'm better at looking after children, though. I've had so much experience at that…

MARILLA hands ANNE her brush, and she begins to scrub.

What's the name of that plant on the window sill?

MARILLA: Apple-scented geranium. I use it for flavouring.

ANNE: I didn't mean that, I meant a *name*. May I call her Bonnie? I mean, just while I'm here?

MARILLA: (*Busy.*) I don't care.

ANNE: I named that cherry-tree outside my window this morning. I called her the Snow Queen. There's so much scope for the imagination here…

MARILLA: Since you're determined to talk, you may as well say something sensible. Tell me about yourself.

ANNE: (*Standing up.*) Can I tell you what I *imagine* about myself?

MARILLA: No. Just you stick to plain facts.

ANNE: My parents were school teachers in Nova Scotia. They died when I was three months old and didn't leave a penny piece. So Mrs Thomas the charlady said she might as well take me. When I was old enough I looked after her four children and her drunken husband, then Mr Thomas was killed falling under a train, and his mother took in Mrs Thomas and the children but she didn't want me, so Mrs Hammond from up river took me as I was handy with children. She had eight of her own. Do you know, she had twins *three times*?

MARILLA: Are you imagining again?

ANNE: Oh no, they were real! I used to get so tired, carrying them about. Anyway, I lived there until they went to the States, and I had to go to the orphan asylum. They didn't want me either, they said they were overcrowded as it was. But they had to take me and then

Mrs Spencer came and that is the end of my true history. But what I *imagine* is –

MARILLA: Those women –

ANNE: Mrs Thomas and Mrs Hammond?

MARILLA: Were they – good to you?

ANNE: (*Hesitant.*) It's very trying to have a drunken husband, and three lots of twins. But still, Miss Cuthbert, I believe in my heart that their intentions were honourable.

MARILLA: The road to hell is paved with good intentions, that's for sure.

MRS PETER BLEWETT enters. MARILLA is surprised and displeased.

Good morning, Mrs Blewett??

MRS BLEWETT: Marilla. This the child?

MARILLA: This is Anne Shirley, Mrs Blewett. What do you want with her?

MATTHEW enters.

Matthew, what's going on?

MRS BLEWETT: A stroke of luck for you, that's what. I've just had to let another servant go – lazy baggage she was, lyin' in bed till six every mornin', eatin' me out of house and home. I was over at Mrs Spencer's, askin' her to go get me an orphan girl, respectful and grateful and used to hard work. Then darn it if Matthew here don't walk right in saying you've got one going spare! I came by to look her over.

MARILLA looks accusingly at MATTHEW as MRS BLEWETT examines ANNE. ANNE flinches at her touch. KATIE, watching too, winces in sympathy.

Hmm – not much to her. Thin – small… (*Feels ANNE's arm.*) But she's wiry – awful wiry. Well, I suppose I'll take her off your hands, Marilla. The baby's terrible fractious, and I'm clean worn out attending to him. I'll expect you to earn your keep, girl, and no mistake. Come along.

ANNE is rooted to the spot.

Look lively there. I've no use for a lazy brat.

ANNE: (*To MATTHEW, in a whisper.*) I shall never forget your kindness to me.

She begins to follow MRS BLEWETT.

MARILLA: Wait.

Everyone, even KATIE, freezes and looks at MARILLA.

I don't know… I didn't say… We hadn't *absolutely* decided… I think it would be best for Matthew and I to talk the matter over, before making a decision. Will that suit you, Mrs Blewett?

MRS BLEWETT: I suppose it'll have to. Send her over this evening if you do make up your mind.

MARILLA: Goodbye, Mrs Blewett.

With a curt nod, MRS BLEWETT leaves.

ANNE: Did you really say I might stay? Or did I just imagine it?

MARILLA: I said we'd talk the matter over. So why don't you sit quietly like a good girl, while we decide?

ANNE: I'll be like anything you want me to, if you'll only let me stay.

ANNE goes out. MARILLA starts scrubbing where MRS BLEWETT left.

MATTHEW: Seems there was a mix-up. Mrs Spencer sent the message by their daughter Nancy, and somewhere along the way she muddled it and asked for a girl.

MARILLA: What do you mean by bringing that woman here?

MATTHEW: I thought you / wanted to send her away.

MARILLA: (*Interrupts.*) You thought! You know I wouldn't give a dog I liked to that Blewett woman! And now it's that, or – Or... (*Sighs.*) Or keeping her ourselves.

MATTHEW: Reckoned you'd come to see it in that light, Marilla.

MARILLA: If we do, you're not to interfere! I will be in charge of Anne, and you're not to stick your oar in.

MATTHEW: There, there, Marilla, you can have it all your own way. Shall I go and tell her that she's staying?

MARILLA: No! You can get back to the dairy. Leave me to speak to Anne.

MATTHEW goes out.

(*Calls after him.*) Perhaps an old maid doesn't know much about children, but I guess I know more than an old bachelor.

ANNE creeps in.

ANNE: Miss Cuthbert...

MARILLA: I suppose I might as well tell you. Matthew and I have decided to keep you – that is, if you'll be a good girl and – whatever's the matter now? I figured you'd be glad to stay!

ANNE: I – I don't know what's wrong with me...

MARILLA: You cry and laugh far too easily, Anne. You must learn to control yourself.

ANNE: Yes, Miss Cuthbert.

MARILLA: And another thing. You'd better stop calling me Miss Cuthbert, it makes me nervous. Call me Marilla.

ANNE: Can I call you Aunt Marilla?

MARILLA: I'm not your aunt.

ANNE: I could imagine you were.

MARILLA looks at the strange girl.

MARILLA: I couldn't.

ANNE: Don't you ever imagine things different from what they are?

MARILLA: No.

ANNE: Oh Marilla, how much you miss! You know, I used to have a bosom friend called Katie Maurice –

MARILLA: I suppose she encouraged you in all this imagining?

ANNE: She couldn't help it. She wasn't really a girl, she was just the reflection in the glass door of Mrs Thomas' bookcase. The other door, not the one that Mr Thomas broke during a fit of intoxication. We used to imagine that the bookcase was enchanted...

KATIE joins ANNE.

ANNE / KATIE: ...and that if I only knew the spell, I could join her in that other land – forever out of reach, but only just beyond the bookcase door.

ANNE: But I never did learn the spell, and then I had to go. It breaks my heart to think of Katie waiting in vain for me to come back. And perhaps one day I will, but I'll have grown up and Katie won't recognise me. Or maybe she'll have grown up, too. What do you think, Marilla?

MARILLA: I think you need to find a real friend.

ANNE: The dream of my life! Do you think it's possible?

MARILLA: Diana Barry lives over at Orchard Slope, and she's about your age. You'll have to be careful though – her mother is very particular.

ANNE: What's Diana like? Is she pretty?

MARILLA: Diana is good and smart, which is better than being pretty.

ANNE: (*Dismayed.*) She's got red hair, hasn't she?

MRS RACHEL LYNDE barges in.

MRS LYNDE: Well, Marilla Cuthbert! I saw Mrs Blewett on the road –

MARILLA: (*Resigned.*) – Of course you did –

MRS LYNDE: – And I've been hearing some surprising things about you!

MARILLA: I haven't got over my own surprise yet.

MRS LYNDE: It's too bad there was such a mistake. But you can't be thinking of *keeping* her?

MARILLA: We thought we'd give her a trial. She's not had an easy life, and – well, Matthew took pity on her.

MRS LYNDE: He didn't pick her for her looks, that's for sure! She's terrible skinny and ugly, Marilla! Come here, child, and let me look at you. (*Chuckles.*) Lawful heart, did anyone ever see such freckles! And hair as red as carrots!

ANNE: I hate you – I hate you! How dare you say such things?

MARILLA: Anne.

ANNE: How would you like to be told that you're fat – and ugly – and old – and haven't a spark of imagination?

MARILLA: Anne!

ANNE: I don't care if I hurt your feelings – I hope I do! You have hurt mine and I'll never forgive you – never!

MARILLA: Anne, go to your room and stay there.

ANNE leaves, white with fury.

MRS LYNDE: Well, there's the end of your "trial", Marilla. Her temper matches her hair, I guess! Don't take it to heart. She'll be better off at the asylum amongst her own kind.

MARILLA: She's never been taught right from wrong. I'll have to give her a good talking-to –

MRS LYNDE: With a birch rod, I hope! That's the only language her sort understand.

MARILLA: You shouldn't have been so hard on her, Rachel.

MRS LYNDE: Well, I'll watch my tongue in future, and be sure to consider the fine feelings of asylum orphans from goodness knows where!

MARILLA: Rachel, don't take offence –

MRS LYNDE: Oh, I'm not angry, Marilla. I'm too sorry for you. But mark this. You'll rue the step you've taken, Marilla Cuthbert, and that's a fact. Good day.

MRS LYNDE storms out.

MARILLA: Anne. Anne!

Lighting change.

Green Gables – Anne's Bedroom

ANNE's bedroom is on a higher level to the rest of Green Gables. MARILLA goes up to join ANNE.

MARILLA: Anne? I was ashamed of you just now, Anne. Thoroughly ashamed.

ANNE: But just imagine how you would feel if –

MARILLA: I've told you before, I don't go around imagining things.

ANNE: What if someone told you to your face that you were ugly? To your *face*, Marilla?

MARILLA: When I was young, I heard my aunts talking about me. Aunt Laura said that I was a very sensible girl. But old Aunt Elizabeth. She said – "What a pity she's such a plain, homely little thing."

ANNE: Oh, Marilla! What did you do?

MARILLA: Nothing. It was true, wasn't it? There are more important things than looks, Anne.

ANNE: But weren't you *humiliated?*

MARILLA: I got over it.

ANNE: I won't. I shall *never* forgive that woman.

MARILLA: Anne, Mrs Lynde was our guest and you should have been respectful to her.

ANNE: *She* should have been respectful to *me!*

MARILLA: You were rude, and you must go and tell her you are very sorry and ask her to forgive you.

ANNE: I can't.

MARILLA: I'm sorry to hear it.

ANNE: I won't do it. Not even if you shut me up in a dark dungeon with snakes and toads, or drag me limb from limb with wild horses.

MARILLA: Dark dungeons and wild horses are rather scarce in Avonlea. But you will apologise to Mrs Lynde, and you will stay in your room until you're willing to do it.

ANNE: I shall have to stay here forever, then. Because I'm not sorry. I can't even imagine that I'm sorry.

MARILLA: Perhaps your imagination will be in better working order by the morning.

MARILLA goes out, leaving ANNE alone. Music.

Green Gables – Kitchen

MATTHEW approaches MARILLA.

MATTHEW: Has she eaten anything?

MARILLA: I'm not in the habit of starving people into good behaviour. I've taken her breakfast, dinner and supper.

MATTHEW: So, has she eaten anything?

MARILLA: (*Reluctant.*) No.

MATTHEW produces a crumpled paper bag.

MATTHEW: I thought maybe some chocolate caramels –

MARILLA: Didn't I say you weren't to stick your oar in? Anne's behaviour was dreadful, and yet you take her part!

MATTHEW: Rachel Lynde is a meddlesome gossip. It's about time someone gave her a calling down.

MARILLA: That may be so, but it's not for Anne to do it.

MATTHEW: I remember, now, when old Aunt Elizabeth –

MARILLA: That was a long time ago.

MARILLA leaves. MATTHEW sneaks off towards ANNE's bedroom.

Green Gables – Anne's Bedroom

MATTHEW: Anne!

ANNE looks up, pleased at the sight of MATTHEW. He offers her the bag of chocolate caramels.

ANNE: Chocolate caramels!

She takes one and pops it into her mouth.

How are you making out?

ANNE: (*With her mouth full of chocolate.*) Pretty well. My imagination helps – I expect in just a few years' time I will have become accustomed to perpetual incarceration.

MATTHEW: Well now, don't you think you'd better just do it and get it over with?

ANNE: You mean – apologise to Mrs Lynde?

MATTHEW: I mean – just sort of smooth it over. It's awful quiet downstairs without you.

He hands ANNE another chocolate caramel.

ANNE: Maybe I *could* do it – to oblige *you*, Matthew.

MATTHEW: That's right – that's right, Anne. But don't tell Marilla.

ANNE: If it's for your sake, I will go to Marilla and declare that I have repented.

MATTHEW hands over the bag and sneaks away.

I shall tell her that I have seen the light, and that I am willing to be taken from this place, to stand before the judgement of Mrs Lynde, and say…

Green Gables – Kitchen

ANNE joins MARILLA and MRS LYNDE. She falls to her knees, and clasps her hands. Music.

ANNE: Oh Mrs Lynde, I could never express my sorrow, not if I used up a whole dictionary. I deserve to be punished and cast out into the eternal darkness forever. That is, unless you will have mercy on an ignorant orphan, and forgive me?

MRS LYNDE: Well… I guess I was a little hard on you…

ANNE: And furthermore. What you said to me was true, every word. What I said was true too, but I shouldn't

29

have said it. Oh Mrs Lynde, if you do not forgive me it will be a lifelong sorrow to me. You wouldn't want to inflict a lifelong sorrow, would you – even onto a wicked, ugly girl with red hair?

MRS LYNDE: There, there, get up, child. Of course I forgive you. I was too outspoken, that's my trouble. Well, it can't be denied – your hair is terrible red – but I knew a girl once with hair as red as yours, and when she grew up it darkened into a real handsome auburn.

ANNE: Oh, Mrs Lynde, you have given me hope. I shall always regard you as a benefactress.

ANNE takes MRS LYNDE's hand and holds it, warmly. It's a reconciliation. MARILLA shakes her head in disbelief. Music.

Green Gables – Kitchen – Later

MRS LYNDE leaves. MATTHEW joins ANNE and MARILLA.

MATTHEW: Well now, is it all over? Did she –

MARILLA: Anne has apologised, all right.

ANNE: I thought since I had to, I might as well do it thoroughly. Do you think my hair will really be auburn when I grow up?

MARILLA: It doesn't matter. Handsome is as handsome does.

ANNE: I've heard that before, but I have my doubts. Still, I have no hard feelings against Mrs Lynde now. How long did it take you to forgive your Aunt Elizabeth, Marilla?

MATTHEW: About forty-five years.

Music.

Green Gables – Kitchen – Some time later

MARILLA holds a new dress up against ANNE.

MARILLA: Well, how do you like it?

ANNE: I'll imagine that I like it.

MARILLA: I don't want you to imagine that you like it!

ANNE: Oh. Then I won't.

MARILLA: Well, put it on, let's see if it fits anyway.

MARILLA helps her into the new dress.

What's wrong with it?

ANNE: It's just that I hoped it would be snow-white muslin, with lace frills and puffed sleeves. I prayed for puffed sleeves, you know. Well, I suppose God didn't have time to bother about a little orphan girl's dress.

MARILLA: No, he didn't. He left it up to me.

ANNE: Oh, Marilla! I'm so sorry – I was so ungrateful. You'd better send me back to the orphan asylum. Of course, I'd probably go into a consumption and die, but that would be better than hurting your feelings.

MARILLA: We'll have no consumptions, if you please! I just want you to behave like other girls. Now, I've got some news for you. Mrs Barry is coming to tea this afternoon and bringing Diana –

ANNE: Diana?! My bosom friend?

MARILLA: Whom you've never met, yes.

ANNE: Oh Marilla, what if she doesn't like me?

MARILLA: I guess she'll like you well enough. It's her mother you've got to reckon with. So when she comes, you be well behaved – and don't make any of your startling speeches. Turn around.

The dress is fastened. ANNE turns around. MARILLA nods.

ANNE: I'm glad I've got a new dress to wear – even if it isn't pretty.

MARILLA: Pretty! No, it isn't. I don't believe in pampering vanity. If something's plain, and neat, and serviceable – that's good enough for me.

ANNE: Except your amethyst brooch.

MARILLA: (*Touching her collar.*) Except my amethyst brooch.

ANNE: I never saw anything so perfectly elegant. May I hold it – just for a minute?

MARILLA: *One* minute.

MARILLA unpins her brooch and hands it to ANNE. ANNE admires it.

ANNE: Do you think amethysts are the souls of good violets?

MARILLA: Christians have souls. Flowers don't.

ANNE: But if they did, I'm sure they'd want to be amethysts. Amethysts are the most beautiful stones. I saw a diamond once, and I was so disappointed. Don't you imagine that diamonds should be purple?

MARILLA: Diamonds are diamonds.

ANNE: Oh, no! They're *symbolic.* Think of *Lancelot and Elaine* and the jousting contest!

MARILLA: (*Sarcastic.*) Oh, I do, all the time.

ANNE holds the brooch up.

ANNE: There was a great jousting contest at Camelot.
Brave Sir Lancelot won, and – the trumpets blew, and all the knights,
His party, cried, "Advance and take thy prize,
The diamond!" – but he answered –

In ANNE's imagination GILBERT, as SIR LANCELOT, enters:

LANCELOT: "Diamond me
No diamonds! for God's love, a little air!
Prize me no prizes, for my prize is death!"

ANNE: He was badly wounded. So they took the diamond to Elaine, because he wore her emblem at the joust. And she went to find him, in the hermit's cave where he lay sick.

KATIE, as ELAINE, joins LANCELOT and gives him the diamond.

ELAINE: Your prize, the diamond sent you by the King.

LANCELOT kisses her cheek. She closes her eyes.

LANCELOT: Alas, your ride hath wearied you. Rest you must have.

ELAINE: Nay, for near you, fair lord, I am at rest.

ANNE: She was in love with him, you see. But he was in love with Guinevere, who was married to King Arthur. And so Lancelot could never marry Elaine.

LANCELOT: (*To ELAINE.*) Had I chosen to wed
I had been wedded earlier, sweet Elaine:
But now there never will be wife of mine.

LANCELOT goes.

ELAINE: He will not love me: how then? Must I die?

MARILLA: (*Interested in spite of herself.*) What did Elaine do?

ANNE: Died, of course. Of a broken heart, naturally.

MARILLA: Naturally.

ANNE: And she sang,

ANNE / ELAINE: *I fain would follow love, if that could be;*
I needs must follow death, who calls for me;
Call and I follow, I follow! let me die!

MARILLA snatches the brooch from ANNE.

MARILLA: (*A little shaken.*) You see, this is exactly the sort of thing that you shouldn't say in front of Mrs Barry!

Music.

Green Gables

MRS BARRY and DIANA arrive. MRS BARRY carries Minnie May.

ANNE: (*Trembling.*) Good afternoon, Mrs Barry. Good afternoon, Diana. (*To the baby.*) Good afternoon –

DIANA: Minnie May.

ANNE: Minnie May.

MRS BARRY: So you are Anne Shirley?

ANNE: Anne with an E.

MRS BARRY: And how are you, Anne with an E?

ANNE: I am well in body although considerably rumpled up in spirit, thank you, ma'am. (*To MARILLA.*) That wasn't startling, was it?

MRS BARRY: (*To MARILLA.*) A most *unusual* child…

MARILLA: Why don't you come into the parlour, Mrs Barry? We'll leave Anne and Diana to get acquainted. (*To MRS BARRY as they go.*) And how is Minnie May?

MARILLA bustles MRS BARRY out, leaving ANNE and DIANA looking bashfully at each other. DIANA breaks the ice.

DIANA: I'm glad you've come to Green Gables. It'll make a change to have a friend my own age.

ANNE: Will you *really* be my friend?

DIANA: I guess so – why not?

ANNE: Will you swear it?

DIANA: It's dreadfully wicked to swear.

ANNE: Not this kind of swearing – it only means to promise faithfully.

DIANA: How do we do it?

ANNE: I'll repeat the oath first. I solemnly swear to be faithful to my bosom friend Diana Barry, as long as the sun and moon shall endure. Now you do it. (*Prompts.*) I solemnly swear –

DIANA: I solemnly swear –

ANNE: To be faithful to my bosom friend Anne Shirley –

DIANA: To be faithful to my bosom friend Anne Shirley. As long as the sun and moon shall endure.

ANNE: (*To DIANA.*) I believe we are kindred spirits. Don't you think so?

DIANA: I – guess. Are you starting at Avonlea school next week?

ANNE: I guess…

DIANA: (*Decides.*) I'm glad.

DIANA takes ANNE's arm and they walk off together. Music.

The Birch Path

DIANA and ANNE, carrying slates, are dawdling on the way to school, down a green, leafy lane.

KATIE watches them.

KATIE: The road to Avonlea school was a little narrow, twisting path, winding down over a long hill, where the light came down through the trees, as flawless as the heart of a diamond…

ANNE: This is one of the prettiest places in the world. What shall we name it?

DIANA: Does *everywhere* need to have a name?

ANNE: Of course! Now, I named Willowmere and Idlewild, and Violet Vale, so it's your turn, Diana.

DIANA: Oh, all right then. (*Looks around.*) I name this path – the Birch Path.

ANNE: The Birch Path?

DIANA: Those are birches. And it's a path.

ANNE: That is certainly accurate.

DIANA: I knew you'd like it. How about the road from your orchard to the woods?

ANNE: That's easy. It has to be Lovers' Lane.

DIANA: I don't know if lovers ever walk there…

ANNE: We could always imagine that they did.

DIANA: Who would you imagine as your lover?

ANNE: It's hard to believe in even imaginary lovers when you've got red hair. How about you?

DIANA: Well. I intend to find a wild, dashing, wicked young man, marry him and reform him…

ANNE: Then I do, too. (*Doubtful.*) I'll have to imagine him, though – I don't know any wild, dashing, wicked young men. Do you?

DIANA: Wait till you meet Gilbert Blythe.

ANNE: Gilbert Blythe?

DIANA: (*Animated.*) He's in the Fifth Reader class. He's *aw'fly* handsome, Anne. And he teases all the girls something terrible. He just torments our lives out. He wrote my name up on the porch wall, last term –

ANNE: No!

DIANA: Yes! He wrote, "Diana Barry and Gilbert Blythe, take notice!"

ANNE: Diana!

DIANA: I know!

ANNE: How mortifying!

DIANA: I know!

ANNE: I should hate to have my name up written up with a boy's! (*Looks at her plait ruefully.*) Not, of course, that anyone would!

An old-fashioned school bell rings in the distance.

DIANA: We're late! Come on!

DIANA sprints off. ANNE dawdles.

Avonlea School

An explosion of energy as the Avonlea School students run, chattering, into the school room and take up their places. DIANA sits alone, there is a spare place next to her. RUBY GILLIS sits in the row behind DIANA. GILBERT BLYTHE sits behind RUBY. They all have slates and slate-pencils.

JOSIE PYE enters and tries to sit down next to DIANA.

DIANA: No, Josie. This seat is taken.

JOSIE: Who by? Your imaginary friend?

DIANA: By my very good *real* friend, Anne Shirley.

JOSIE: So where is she?

DIANA: (*Looks to the door.*) I... She was with me just a moment ago...

RUBY: Teacher's coming! Ssh!

MISS STACY enters. A disgruntled JOSIE sits next to RUBY.

MISS STACY: I'll be a little longer with my Queen's scholars. Those of you in the Fourth Reader class, look at your recital pieces for the school concert.

She leaves.

JOSIE: You know, that Anne Shirley's awful strange.

DIANA: You don't even know her!

JOSIE: Who cares? You should hear the stories they're telling about her in the village!

GILBERT: (*Interested.*) What stories?

RUBY: Mrs Lynde says she's got a fearsome temper.

DIANA: She has a passionate spirit.

JOSIE: Jerry Buote says she talks to the trees and flowers like a crazy girl.

DIANA: That's her imagination. Too bad you haven't got one, Josie.

ANNE enters and becomes the focus of everyone's attention. She's stuck wild flowers into the brim of her hat. JOSIE and RUBY immediately begin to laugh, DIANA is embarrassed, GILBERT intrigued.

Anne – over here.

JOSIE: Ain't you going to take your hat off, *Anne?*

DIANA: Anne!

DIANA mimes "hat" to ANNE. ANNE feels along her hat, and remembers the flowers.

ANNE: (*To DIANA.*) I'm sorry. I saw the buttercups and I couldn't resist them – I wanted to make a garland of flowers – so romantic, you know?

JOSIE snorts.

JOSIE: What a scarecrow!

DIANA: (*Loyal.*) I think you look beautiful, Anne.

JOSIE: (*To GILBERT.*) I can't *believe* Di Barry's new friend, can you?

GILBERT: She's certainly – different.

JOSIE: Exactly!

GILBERT: Anne! Anne!

ANNE turns round. GILBERT winks at ANNE.

ANNE: Did that boy just *wink* at me?

RUBY: (*Disappointed.*) I thought it was at me.

MISS STACY comes over, with a warm smile of greeting.

MISS STACY: You must be Anne Shirley?

ANNE: Anne with an / E.

MISS STACY: – E. I know.

ANNE: I felt instinctively that you did.

MISS STACY: Marilla says you've read a great deal?

ANNE: Not really. I didn't get to go to school much. But I know *The Dog at his Master's Grave* – that's so tragical, and *Lancelot and Elaine* – that just gives me shivers all over.

JOSIE: (*Aside to GILBERT.*) What on *earth* does she mean?

GILBERT: (*Intrigued.*) I'd love to know.

MISS STACY: Well, you're the first student of mine who ever read Tennyson by choice! Maybe I should move you to the Fifth Reader class?

ANNE: Oh, no! I want to sit here with my bosom friend Diana Barry. And besides, I'm an awful dunce at mathematics.

MISS STACY: Very well, Anne. You stay here and we'll see how you do.

MISS STACY leaves. The students write on their slates.

GILBERT: Anne! Anne!

ANNE looks around. GILBERT is tying JOSIE's braid to her chair. He taps her on the opposite shoulder. She looks round, and falls back onto her chair.

JOSIE: Ow!!

The class laugh. JOSIE glares at GILBERT.

GILBERT: Anne! Talk to me, Anne!

ANNE ignores him. DIANA nudges her.

DIANA: Anne, Gilbert wants you.

ANNE: Well, I don't want him.

DIANA: Don't you think he's handsome?

ANNE: Maybe, but he's awfully rude.

DIANA: It's only Josie Pye. She deserves it.

ANNE: Well, I call it ungentlemanly.

GILBERT: Anne! Anne Shirley! That's your name ain't it?

DIANA giggles but ANNE doesn't react.

Carrots! Hey, Carrots!

GILBERT gets up and pulls ANNE's plait.

Carrots!!

ANNE turns round to GILBERT.

ANNE: You mean boy! How *dare* you!

ANNE smacks him over the head with her slate. It cracks. GILBERT is dazed.

ALL SCHOLARS: (*Delighted.*) Oooh !

DIANA: Anne! How could you?

ANNE is crying with anger.

ANNE: I – he – CARROTS!

ANNE rushes from the room.

GILBERT: Anne!

GILBERT chases out after ANNE.

Anne!

JOSIE: Ooh! Gilbert's going to fight Anne Shirley!

DIANA: No! Gilbert! Anne!

DIANA follows ANNE and GILBERT.

RUBY: I wanna see the fight!

RUBY / JOSIE / OTHER SCHOLARS: Fight! Fight! Fight!

All the students run off, excited.

Outside Avonlea School

GILBERT catches ANNE.

GILBERT: Anne! Anne, wait!

He takes ANNE's arm. She shakes him off.

I'm sorry I made fun of your hair. Honest I am. Don't be mad for keeps, now.

Behind GILBERT, DIANA enters. ANNE freezes GILBERT out with a terrible look, and walks past him.

ANNE: Diana. Tell Gilbert Blythe I shall never forgive him.

ANNE walks off. RUBY and JOSIE run in.

RUBY: (*Disappointed.*) Did we miss the fight?

GILBERT storms past the girls.

DIANA: (*To herself, admiring.*) Oh, how could you, Anne?

Outside Green Gables

MRS LYNDE and MARILLA.

MRS LYNDE: Well, she's certainly caused a sensation at Avonlea school! Will Miss Stacy take her back, do you think?

MARILLA: She doesn't have a choice. Anne won't go back to school. She says she's been "insulted." The "iron has entered her soul". Apparently. What have I taken on, Rachel?

MRS LYNDE: If you'll take my advice, Marilla – which I suppose you won't do, although I've brought up ten children and buried two – if you ask my advice, Marilla –

MARILLA: Rachel, I am.

MRS LYNDE: Oh… I'd humour her a little, that's all.

MARILLA: *Really?*

MRS LYNDE: Depend upon it, she'll cool off in a week or so. But if you try and force her back, she'll make more trouble than ever.

MARILLA: (*Relieved.*) Do you know, Rachel – I believe you're right.

MRS LYNDE: She actually broke a slate over that Blythe boy's head?

MARILLA: I don't think she hurt him. His pride, perhaps.

MRS LYNDE: I saw Gilbert at the church picnic… He seems so tall and manly. How time flies. Nice-looking young fellow, too.

MARILLA: Handsome is as handsome does.

MRS LYNDE: (*Fishing.*) He looks like his father…

MARILLA: Yes, Rachel.

MRS LYNDE: You know, I always wondered…

MARILLA: I'm sure you did. (*Beat.*) It was a silly quarrel. I wouldn't forgive him when he asked me. I always meant to, eventually… but he never came back. The Blythes were always mighty stubborn.

MRS LYNDE: They're not the only ones.

Music.

Green Gables – Later

MARILLA: Anne? Anne!

ANNE slopes in, miserable.

Anne, I've decided – you may stay home from school if you like, but mind you learn your lessons at home –

ANNE: (*Sadly.*) Thank you, Marilla.

MARILLA: Why Anne, whatever's wrong *now*? You're not still crying about what Gilbert Blythe said –

ANNE: Never mention that person to me!

MARILLA: So it was him?

ANNE: No! (*Upset.*) I was just thinking about – Diana.

MARILLA: Has *she* upset you now?

ANNE: Oh, no. Diana is my best friend in the world. I cannot live without her. But when we grow up, she'll get married, and go away, and leave me… (*In tears.*) And I shall be bridesmaid, in a lovely dress with puffed sleeves, but underneath, my heart will be breaking…

MARILLA bursts out laughing.

MARILLA: Oh, Anne!

ANNE: Marilla?

MARILLA: If you must borrow trouble, for pity's sake borrow it handier home! Diana won't be married for years!

ANNE: But now I cannot see her even in school – not while *that person* is there…

MARILLA looks at ANNE with sympathy and makes a sudden decision.

MARILLA: Would you like to invite Diana over for tea, tomorrow?

ANNE: Oh, Marilla! Can I really?

MARILLA: I just said so, didn't I? Now, I'm going to the Aid Society meeting, and Matthew will be picking potatoes, so you'll have Green Gables to yourselves. There's a bottle of raspberry cordial in the closet – you and Diana can share it.

ANNE: Oh, thank you, Marilla! I love bright red drinks, don't you? They taste twice as good as any other colour!

MARILLA shakes her head with good humour and leaves.

Green Gables – Kitchen –Later

DIANA joins ANNE. The two shake hands with excessive formality.

ANNE: Good afternoon, Miss Barry. Do allow me to take your hat.

DIANA: Thank you, Miss Shirley.

ANNE takes DIANA's hat. DIANA sits.

(*Forgetting to be formal.*) I wish you'd come back to school, Anne! I hate sitting with Josie Pye. And school's *ever* so interesting at the moment. Josie wrote her name up in a "Take Notice" with Gilbert Blythe's. And you'll never guess what Gilbert did –

ANNE: (*Interrupting.*) Would you care for a glass of raspberry cordial Miss Barry?

DIANA: I would care for it indeed.

ANNE: Good! Let's drink it right away!

ANNE fetches a bottle of cordial and pours two tumblers full. ANNE looks at hers dreamily.

It's almost too beautiful to taste. Like drinking rubies.

DIANA takes a big slurp.

DIANA: That's awfully nice raspberry cordial, Anne.

ANNE: I'm glad you like it. Take as much as you want.

ANNE tops up DIANA's cordial glass and takes a dainty sip from her own.

DIANA: (*Guzzles the cordial.*) This is ever so much nicer than Mrs Lynde's cordial.

ANNE: I should think so! Marilla is a famous cook!

DIANA drains her glass and holds it out for more. ANNE fills it up.

She's trying to teach me to cook, but it's uphill work. The last time I made a cake, I forgot to put the flour in. Whoever would have thought flour was so essential to cakes?

DIANA pours herself yet more cordial.

I couldn't help forgetting the flour – I was thinking up the loveliest story, Diana. You were desperately ill with the smallpox, and deserted by all. But I went boldly to your bedside and nursed you back to life, and then I took the smallpox and died and you planted a rose-bush by my grave and watered it with your tears and you never forgot the friend of your youth.

DIANA: And I never will. I never will forget you, Anne.

DIANA clasps ANNE's hand.

ANNE: I know. Please have some more cordial.

DIANA pours more cordial – quite unsteadily.

DIANA: I never knew raspberry cordial was so nice.

ANNE: I'm terribly forgetful, myself. The other day, I forgot to cover the pudding sauce, and a mouse drowned in it. Then I forgot about *that*, until the minister came to tea and I saw Marilla come in with the pitcher of mouse sauce, all nicely warmed up. And I just stood and shrieked – "Don't eat that, there's a mouse drowned in it!"

DIANA giggles uncontrollably.

Marilla gave me such a scolding. But at least I only did it once. I can only hope that one day I'll have made every single possible mistake and there won't be any more left. Your glass is empty, Miss Barry – allow me – oh, or help yourself.

DIANA: (*Pouring.*) This is the nicest drank I ever drink.

ANNE: Diana?

DIANA: I mean, it's the best drunk I drank... I. I feel dizzy.

ANNE: Oh dear... Finish your cordial, it should revive you.

DIANA raises the cordial glass to her lips, drunkenly. She knocks it back and slumps onto the table.

Diana! Dear Diana, wake up!

DIANA lifts her head up. She sees ANNE and KATIE.

DIANA: Anne! Stop – stop moving… you're making me… Stand still.

DIANA collapses again.

ANNE: I'm right here, Diana.

DIANA: I'm awful sick. I have to go home.

ANNE: But you haven't had your tea!

DIANA stands, hiccups and falls over.

Diana – Diana, what's wrong?

DIANA, on the floor, burps loudly. She begins giggling to herself.

Oh Diana, you're delirious.

DIANA: Take me home.

ANNE: Of course I will.

ANNE helps DIANA to her feet. Music. Lighting change.

Outside the Barrys' House

KATIE: With tears in her eyes, Anne helped Diana as far as the Barry yard fence.

ANNE is supporting DIANA, who is swinging about wildly, falling over.

ANNE: Diana, I don't know if you can understand me, but I'll say it anyway. If you really are afflicted with a mortal illness, I promise to nurse you back to health, even should I be stricken down myself.

DIANA: Need to lie down…

ANNE: No! Diana, do not give up all hope… we're almost there…

MRS BARRY meets the girls.

MRS BARRY: Diana! What's the matter?

DIANA begins to giggle.

ANNE: Diana has been taken ill. I fear she may be delirious.

MRS BARRY: Delirious?

DIANA: 'S all spinny.

MRS BARRY goes to DIANA and feels her forehead. She smells something on DIANA's breath and frowns.

MRS BARRY: I think you'd better go, Anne.

ANNE: But I can't leave my bosom friend like this!

MRS BARRY: Your *what?*

DIANA: Bosom friend. That's what she said. Bosom friend. Swore it. I did. She taught me to swear. I love Anne.

MRS BARRY: Girls, have you been *drinking*?

ANNE: Yes, raspberry cordial.

DIANA: She gave me three big glasses full… let me drink the whole bottle.

MRS BARRY: Anne! Is this true?

ANNE: Why, ma'am – yes, it is.

MRS BARRY: (*Stern.*) Get away from my daughter.

DIANA is noisily sick.

ANNE: Oh, please, Mrs Barry, don't send me away! What if Diana's taken the smallpox –

MRS BARRY: *Smalpox?* She's *drunk*, that's what she is –
plain as plain!

DIANA: Mother, am I gonna die?

MRS BARRY: No, dear. This wicked child has set you
drunk, that's all.

DIANA: (*Confused.*) Drunk…?

MRS BARRY: (*To DIANA.*) Drunk.

ANNE: Drunk! ?

MRS BARRY: (*Infuriated.*) Drunk!

MARILLA: (*Enters.*) Drunk!

MATTHEW: (*Enters.*) *Drunk?*

MRS BARRY and DIANA exit. Lighting change to:

Green Gables – Kitchen

*ANNE, MARILLA, MATTHEW. MARILLA examines the
empty cordial bottle.*

ANNE: (*Miserable.*) Drunk.

MARILLA: Anne Shirley, you have a genius for trouble.
Don't you know the difference between cordial and
currant wine?

ANNE: I never tasted either. It seems that the stars in their
courses fight against me. Diana and I are parted forever.

MARILLA: Don't be foolish. Mrs Barry will cool off in
time. You just go on over there and tell her it was an
accident.

ANNE: Her wrath was very great. I fear my courage shall
fail me.

MATTHEW: Just do whatever you did to Rachel Lynde.

ANNE: I will, Matthew. Thank you. Oh, how little I dreamed of this when first we swore our vows of friendship.

ANNE goes out. MATTHEW laughs, and looks at MARILLA, who looks serious.

MATTHEW: Well now Marilla, I'm sure it was an innocent mistake.

MARILLA: There have been a few too many "mistakes" around here since she came. Let's hope this is the last .

MARILLA goes out, carrying the bottle. MATTHEW follows, looking concerned.

Outside the Barrys' House

MRS BARRY looks on unsympathetically as ANNE delivers the climax of one of her speeches. DIANA stands to the side with her baby sister Minnie May.

ANNE: I thought it was only raspberry cordial. I was firmly convinced it was raspberry cordial. Oh Mrs Barry, please forgive me, or you will cover my life with a dark cloud of woe.

MRS BARRY: I don't think you are a fit person for Diana and Minnie May to associate with. Please go now, Anne Shirley.

ANNE glances at DIANA.

Did you hear me?

ANNE: Won't you even let us say farewell?

DIANA: Mother, please…?

MRS BARRY: Two minutes.

ANNE: That's not very long for an eternal farewell.

MRS BARRY: I'll time you by the clock.

MRS BARRY goes out, with Minnie. DIANA joins ANNE.

DIANA: I cried and cried and I told her it wasn't your fault, but –

ANNE: I know. She will not relent.

DIANA: (*Sobbing.*) I'll never have another bosom friend – nobody could ever replace you.

ANNE: Nor you. In the long years to come, thy memory will shine like a star over my lonely life. Oh, Diana, wilt thou give me a lock of thy jet-black tresses to treasure for evermore?

DIANA: Have you – hast thou got anything to cutteth it with?

ANNE: Yes, fortunately I was prepared for this eventuality.

ANNE produces scissors from her apron pocket and cuts a lock of DIANA's hair.

Henceforth we must be as strangers, though living side by side. But my heart will ever be devoted to thee.

MRS BARRY appears, gesturing that time is up. DIANA goes to her.

DIANA: Then I guess this is goodbye, Anne.

ANNE: Fare thee well, Diana.

Music.
The BARRY family leave. ANNE looks wistfully after them.
Music and cross-fade to:

The Classroom

KATIE's reading to MR CARR.

KATIE: Mrs Barry was a woman of strong prejudices, and her anger was of the cold sort which is always hardest to overcome.

MR CARR: So that was it? She wouldn't forgive her, even when she apologised?

MARIAN enters, and regards KATIE with suspicion.

MARIAN: You still here?

KATIE: (*On her dignity.*) I was just leaving…

MR CARR: Those girls should be long gone by now. (*To KATIE.*) Tell me if they give you any trouble.

KATIE: Thank you.

MR CARR goes.

MARIAN: (*Hostile, to KATIE.*) You'd best be off then. And mind how you go on your way out – I'll be watching you.

KATIE: (*Amazed.*) What do you think I will do?

MARIAN: We'll have none of your cheek. Just go.

KATIE and MARIAN leave.

Green Gables

ANNE talks to an unseen MATTHEW and MARILLA.

ANNE: It is all over. I shall never have another friend, and now I'm worse off than ever for I haven't even Katie Maurice. Diana and I had such an affecting farewell. She gave me a lock of her hair and I'm going to sew it up in a bag and wear it around my neck all my life. Please see that it is buried with me, for I don't believe I'll live very long. Perhaps when she sees me lying cold and dead before her, Mrs Barry will feel remorse for the wrong she has done and will let Diana come to my funeral. She might, mightn't she, Marilla… Marilla? What's wrong?

MARILLA: (*Enters, disturbed.*) Anne, have you seen my amethyst brooch?

ANNE: Yes... I saw it this afternoon... I went to your room and I – I pinned it on my dress, just to see how it would look –

MARILLA: Go on.

ANNE: That's it. I put it back on the bureau.

MARILLA: You didn't put it back. That brooch isn't anywhere in the room, Anne.

ANNE: Marilla, you don't – you can't think I / took it?

MARILLA: / If you put it back it's there still. If it isn't –

ANNE: I put it back. It will be there. It must be.

MATTHEW: (*To MARILLA.*) You're sure it hasn't fell down behind the bureau?

MARILLA: I've moved the bureau and I've taken out the drawers and searched every nook and cranny. The brooch is gone. Now Anne, what have you done with it?

ANNE: I never took the brooch out of your room, and that is the truth, if I were to be led to the block for it. And I'm not even sure what a block is.

MARILLA: Are you sure what a lie is?

ANNE: Yes!

MARILLA: Go to your room, Anne. And stay there until you're ready to tell me what you've done with my brooch.

ANNE: Marilla, I know you're angry but please believe me –

MARILLA: Is this your confession?

ANNE: No!

MARILLA: Then I don't want to hear it.

ANNE looks at MARILLA, closes her lips tightly and walks out.

MATTHEW: Have you looked in the, er…

MARILLA: I've searched everywhere. She's taken it, Matthew, and she'll stay in her room until she confesses.

MATTHEW: Worked last time, didn't it?

Unseen by MATTHEW and MARILLA, ANNE is listening.

MARILLA: I don't suppose she meant to steal. Maybe just wanted to help along that "imagination." (*Pause.*) Matthew – I've put up with a lot from Anne, but this… I don't know if we can keep her after this. (*Pause.*) You know, I wouldn't mind so much – if she'd only confessed.

ANNE re-enters.

ANNE: Marilla? I'm – ready, now.

MARILLA: Then let's hear what you have to say.

ANNE: I took the amethyst brooch. I took it just as you said. I was going to put it back, but then I thought how thrilling it would be…

GILBERT and KATIE enter, as LANCELOT and ELAINE.

…to imagine I was the Lady Elaine, with the diamond given to me by Sir Lancelot. I stood on the bridge by the lake, and I came to the part when Elaine dreams, "That someone put this diamond in her hand, –

ELAINE: (*Enacting the scene.*) And that it was too slippery to be held,
And – slipped and fell into some pool or stream…"

ANNE: But I guess I imagined too well, for the brooch just slipped through my fingers – and down it fell, all purply-sparkling, and sank forever more to the very bottom of the Lake of Shining Waters. Nevermore to be seen in this world.

Pause. GILBERT and KATIE exit.

ANNE seems uplifted, rather than otherwise, by her story. MARILLA sees this.

MARILLA: (*Flat.*) That brooch belonged to my mother. It was the only thing I had to remember her by.

ANNE: I didn't know / it was your mother's –

MARILLA: / Well, now you do.

MATTHEW: (*Hastily.*) And I'm sure she's sorry for it, ain't you, Anne?

ANNE: Oh – yes. I *do* feel sorry – so *excruciatingly* sorry –

MARILLA: Oh no. Not again.

MATTHEW and ANNE are silenced.

Anne, I didn't want to send you to Mrs Blewett, but I can't cope with you and that's a fact. I think – you'll have to go back to Nova Scotia.

ANNE: You are pronouncing a sentence of death.

MARILLA: Stuff and nonsense!

ANNE: I can't leave Green Gables, not now. I just can't.

MARILLA: You should have thought of that before you stole.

ANNE: *Marilla* – please –

MARILLA: And lied. It's the lying, most of all, Anne.

ANNE is silenced.

(*Without looking at ANNE.*) Go to your room and pack.

ANNE goes.

MATTHEW: She's had a hard life. We should make allowances –

MARILLA: I made all the allowances I could. We tried, and failed. That's all.

Music.
KATIE, with a bag, makes her way out. She crosses ANNE,
also making her way across the stage.

Song: "Wayfaring Stranger"

FULL COMPANY:
> *I'm just a poor wayfaring stranger,*
> *A-travellin' through this world of woe*
> *But there's no sickness, toil or danger*
> *In that bright world to which I go.*
> *I'm goin' there to meet my father,*
> *I'm goin' there, no more to roam.*
> *I'm just a-going over Jordan,*
> *I'm just a-going over home.*

End of Act One.

ACT TWO

The Classroom

The school bell rings insistently. Modern RUBY and JOSIE are waiting.

KATIE comes tearing in and is stopped by JOSIE.

JOSIE: Where's the fire?

KATIE: I do not –

JOSIE: Don't give me that "don't understand". You understand about handouts all right, don't you? (*Looks at KATIE's clothes.*) Shame you don't understand fashion.

RUBY giggles. JOSIE pushes KATIE. MR CARR interrupts them.

MR CARR: Is there a problem here, girls?

JOSIE: Yeah, you, Grandad.

RUBY: (*Mutters, to JOSIE.*) Just leave it, yeah?

JOSIE: (*To KATIE.*) Is he your boyfriend? That's disgustin'.

MR CARR: I'll tell you what is disgusting. The way you gang up on this lass, that's what. I've got my eye on you, young lady. So watch it.

JOSIE: You're not the boss of us. You're just a cleaner.

MR CARR: That's right. Time I sorted out some of the rubbish around here.

MR CARR splashes JOSIE with his mop, getting dirty water down her coat. She squeals.

JOSIE: I'm getting my dad on you!

JOSIE runs off, followed by a somewhat amused RUBY.

KATIE: Will you be in trouble?

MR CARR: Don't worry about her. All talk and no trousers, that sort. (*He winces in pain.*)

KATIE: Are you hurt?

MR CARR: No – not as young as I was, that's all. (*Changing the subject.*) By the way – wouldn't mind seeing how that book turned out.

Lighting change. KATIE narrates. MR CARR goes.

KATIE: It was a dismal morning at Green Gables. Marilla worked fiercely and scrubbed the porch door and the dairy shelves. Neither the shelves nor the porch needed it – but Marilla did.

Green Gables – Kitchen

A miserable ANNE waits with her coat, hat and carpet bag. MARILLA cleans fiercely.

MARILLA: Get along there Anne, Matthew's waiting with the buggy.

ANNE: Marilla, aren't you coming to the station?

MARILLA: (*Busy.*) And why would I want to do that?

ANNE: To say goodbye?

MARILLA: Get on outside, I'll fetch my shawl and join you.

ANNE exits. MARILLA gets her shawl. As she does so, she notices something. The brooch is pinned to the shawl. She examines the brooch.

Anne! Anne! Matthew!

ANNE returns, followed by MATTHEW.

Anne Shirley! What do you call this?

ANNE: (*Very dejected.*) It's your amethyst brooch, Marilla.

MARILLA: Yes, I found it stuck to my shawl. And you told me it was at the bottom of Barry's pond!

ANNE: I wanted to go to the picnic, and you wanted me to confess. So I made up the most interesting confession I could.

MARILLA: I was going to send you away! Why didn't you –

ANNE: You said lying was worse than stealing.

MARILLA: Well, so it is – sometimes – but – well, I suppose I drove you to it. Of course, it wasn't right for you to confess to a thing you hadn't done – in fact, it was very wrong. But I'll forgive you – if you'll forgive me, Anne.

ANNE flies at MARILLA and hugs her. MARILLA's almost knocked off her feet.

ANNE: Thank you, Marilla, thank you! You're so good to me!

ANNE kisses MARILLA's cheek.

MARILLA: (*Taken aback.*) There, there, never mind your kissing nonsense. We'll forgive each other and start square again – that's all there is to it.

ANNE: And I can stay at Green Gables?

MARILLA: You can stay at Green Gables.

ANNE: My happiness is beyond words.

ANNE runs off.

MARILLA: Go on, then. Say "I told you so." You were right, to trust her, and I was wrong.

MATTHEW: Just as you say, Marilla.

MARILLA: I shall never understand that child – but maybe she'll turn out all right yet.

Music.

Avonlea School

The old-fashioned school bell rings. All the Avonlea scholars come charging in – GILBERT, RUBY, JOSIE and DIANA. ANNE arrives last.

GILBERT: Anne! You're back!

She ignores him.

What's wrong? You're not still mad about what I said are you?

RUBY: Anne! Didn't you hear Gilbert?

ANNE: Who?

MISS STACY enters with books and papers.

MISS STACY: Why, Anne Shirley! I didn't expect to see you here.

ANNE: School is all I have left, now that my bosom friend and I have been torn asunder.

ANNE looks hopefully over to DIANA, who stares straight through her.

RUBY: You can sit with me, Anne.

ANNE sits down next to RUBY. As she passes –

JOSIE: Look out! She's got a slate!

MISS STACY: Very funny, Josie. Nearly as amusing as your essay on English History. Which I would like you to write again, as a Roman Centurion is *not* a "hundred year old Italian."

JOSIE takes the essay back from MISS STACY.

I'm glad you decided to give us another chance, Anne.

ANNE: Miss Stacy, can you ever forgive me?

MISS STACY: It's all right, Anne. Gilbert explained everything. He took all the blame upon himself.

ANNE: Oh. And so he should.

MISS STACY: (*Hands out books.*) I remember you said you enjoyed Tennyson, Anne?

JOSIE: *Poetry!*

MISS STACY: We'll be studying a great deal more poetry this term.

Groans from the class.

You'll all need to widen your reading if you're to try for places at Queen's College.

JOSIE: But the exams aren't for ages!

MISS STACY: It's never too early to start. Open your books at page seventeen and start reading – quietly!

ANNE: *Lancelot and Elaine!*

GILBERT: Anne!

GILBERT passes ANNE a crumpled piece of paper. She opens it.

RUBY: A candy heart! Oh, that means he wants you to be his sweetheart!

ANNE turns around and sees GILBERT. He winks at her. ANNE crushes the heart beneath her heel.

ANNE: I'm nobody's "sweetheart".

JOSIE: Avonlea boys not good enough for you, Queen Anne?

ANNE: I prefer to concentrate on my education. I mean to try for Queen's college, you know.

JOSIE: I don't think you'd fit in. They use slates for writing, not fighting.

RUBY: Don't be mean, Josie.

JOSIE: Hey, Diana! Ain't you sticking up for your *friend?*

DIANA: Mother says I'm not to talk to Anne Shirley, so I'm not. But you're still a fat ugly pig, Josie Pye, and I can tell you *that.*

JOSIE: You're awful cross, Diana. What's wrong? Did you have too much to drink last night?

MISS STACY: That's enough, Josie! We all make mistakes – you of all people should know that. The important thing is to forgive each other and get on with our lives.

GILBERT looks hopefully over at ANNE but she ignores him.

And our studies. Gilbert, would you start reading?

GILBERT opens his book, too.

GILBERT: Elaine the fair, Elaine the loveable,
Elaine, the lily maid of Astolat,
High in her chamber up a tower to the east
Guarded the sacred shield of Lancelot…

As GILBERT reads, we see KATIE as ELAINE. Music over scene change.

Green Gables – Kitchen

ANNE sits working. MATTHEW is smoking his pipe.

ANNE: Matthew, did you ever study geometry?

MATTHEW: Well now, no, I didn't.

ANNE: You're so lucky. It's casting a cloud over my whole life.

MATTHEW: Miss Stacy says you're the smartest scholar in school.

ANNE: Really? Because most people think that Gil – one of the boys is the smartest – (*Hurriedly.*) I wonder how Marilla and Mrs Lynde are enjoying themselves at the rally? Mrs Lynde says the country's going to the dogs and the Premier ought to be told. Didn't you want to go, Matthew?

MATTHEW: Not to Charlottetown. That place is too big for me.

ANNE: Everyone else will be there, Mrs Lynde says. Mrs Lynde is a red-hot politician. She says if women were allowed to vote we would soon see a blessed change. Don't you agree, Matthew?

MATTHEW: It's just as you say, now, Anne.

DIANA comes running in, upset.

ANNE: Diana!

DIANA: Anne…

ANNE: Why, Diana, whatever is the matter?

DIANA: Minnie May is awful sick – I think it's croup – and Father and Mother have gone to the rally – and there's nobody to go for the doctor –

MATTHEW: Well, now – I'll go.

MATTHEW jumps up and goes.

DIANA: She's awful bad, Anne…

ANNE: Don't cry, Diana. I know just what to do. Just let me get a few things and we'll go straight over.

The girls hurry out. Music.

The Barry House

DIANA and ANNE are bent over a cradle containing Minnie May.

ANNE: It's the croup all right. Not ordinary croup either.

DIANA sobs.

But I've seen worse. Mrs Hammond's twins all had croup regularly. Now, we need lots of hot water – and I brought the ipecac.

ANNE hands DIANA the bottle of ipecac.

Can you give her that?

DIANA bends over the crib. Coughing and spluttering noises. DIANA gestures helplessly.

DIANA: She won't take it.

ANNE: I'll do it. You go and build up the fire, now. And boil the kettle…

DIANA goes off. ANNE picks up Minnie May and sternly administers the medicine.

Oh, Minnie May. You're sicker than ever the Hammond twins were, and you must take this. There now. Cough – there's a good girl… That's right. Ssh, ssh.

Music and lighting change.
Hours later.

That's the last of the ipecac.

ANNE sits down, exhausted. DIANA takes Minnie May.

DIANA: Anne… I think she's choking.

ANNE: Choking?

ANNE jumps up and runs to her.

She's not breathing.

DIANA: (*Frightened.*) Anne, what are we going to do?

ANNE: (*Thinks.*) Is there any sulphur in the house, Diana?

DIANA: Yes, but –

ANNE: Then get it! Hurry!

DIANA goes.

(*Patting Minnie May's back.*) This is the last lingering hope, Minnie May, and I fear 'tis a vain one. But we won't tell Diana, will we? Good girl.

DIANA returns.

Got it? Now, throw a spoonful on the fire.

ANNE ties her apron around her mouth. DIANA throws the sulphur onto the "fire" and a cloud of choking smoke billows up. DIANA coughs and chokes. ANNE holds Minnie May over the stove.

DIANA: Anne – don't! You'll choke her!

ANNE: (*Through the apron.*) She's choking anyway!

ANNE sits down with Minnie.

DIANA: How – how is she?

ANNE: There was a membrane in her throat. Choking her. She's coughed it up now.

An exhausted ANNE sits back, cuddling Minnie May. DIANA joins them.

DIANA: Oh, Minnie May! I – I'm so relieved – I can't begin to tell you. How on earth did you know about the sulphur?

ANNE: It was Mrs Hammond's old grandmother's remedy.

DIANA: Mother would never have let you. She'd have called it an old wives' trick.

ANNE: I guess old wives must know some things.

MRS BARRY enters.

MRS BARRY: Anne Shirley!

MRS BARRY snatches Minnie from ANNE.

Diana. What is this person doing here?

ANNE: I was just leaving, Mrs Barry.

ANNE leaves.

DIANA: Mother, you don't understand!

MRS BARRY: No, I don't understand why you disobeyed me, Diana!

DIANA: Look at Minnie May!

MRS BARRY looks at Minnie May as MATTHEW enters.

Oh, Matthew! Have you brought the doctor?

MATTHEW: He's on his way. Sorry I took so long – had to go all the way over to Charlottetown to find him. (*Awkward.*) How's the – the little 'un?

DIANA: (*Breaking down.*) We thought she was dying…

MRS BARRY is shocked.

She was choking to death with the croup. Anne saved her life.

MRS BARRY: *Anne* saved her?

MATTHEW: Of course she did.

MRS BARRY is speechless.

Well now – where *is* Anne?

DIANA looks accusingly at her mother. Music and lighting change.

The Barrys' House – Next morning

DIANA and Minnie May as they were when ANNE apologised. MRS BARRY and ANNE's positions are reversed.

MRS BARRY: By the time Doctor Blair got here, it would have been too late. He told me that… You saved Minnie May's life, Anne.

ANNE waits for MRS BARRY to continue.

I know now you didn't mean to set Diana drunk. I – I don't know how to repay you.

ANNE still waits before reacting, very much on her dignity.

I am sorry I acted as I did, and – And I hope you'll forgive me and be friends with Diana again.

ANNE: I have no hard feelings for you, Mrs Barry, I assure you. Henceforth, let us cover the past with the mantle of oblivion.

MRS BARRY kisses a startled ANNE on the cheek. Music.

The Classroom

KATIE: Anne came dancing home across the snow, with a song in her heart and on her lips.

MARIAN bustles in.

MARIAN: That little horror says you attacked her with a mop!

MR CARR: You know these girls – vivid imaginations.

MARIAN: Well, you want to watch yourself. Her dad's a school governor. She says. And what are you doing now? Reading some kids' book?

MR CARR: There's nowt wrong with enjoying a good story.

MARIAN: That's your trouble, isn't it? You just don't live in the real world!

MARIAN walks off.

MR CARR: (*To KATIE.*) Now, why on earth would I want to do that?

Music.

Avonlea School

Lunchtime. ANNE, DIANA and RUBY are alone in the schoolroom.

DIANA: You don't have to join if you don't want to, Ruby.

RUBY: (*Whining.*) I *do* want to. I just don't know why we have to write stories out of our own heads.

ANNE: (*Waves a piece of paper.*) The Avonlea Story Club Constitution clearly states that each member must produce one story a week.

RUBY: Well, all right then, but why can't we – ?

ANNE: No!

RUBY: I just think –

ANNE / DIANA: No!

RUBY: Having boys in the club would make it so much more exciting.

ANNE: The purpose of the Story Club is to cultivate our imaginations.

DIANA: Not to chase the men, Ruby.

ANNE: Anyway, let us proceed. "The Jealous Rival, or, "In Death Not Divided."

JOSIE PYE enters.

JOSIE: Who's jealous? What's going on?

DIANA: Nothing to do with you.

JOSIE: I know you're up to something. (*Picks up ANNE's paper.*) The Avonlea Story Club! So, what – you sit here and tell stories?

DIANA: You should hear Anne's stories. They're thrilling.

JOSIE: I guess she lies well. All orphans are liars and thieves.

DIANA: Anne's not!

ANNE: Do you want to hear a *true* story, Josie?

JOSIE: I suppose I may as well.

ANNE: Once, far across the sea in Nova Scotia, I worked for Mr Thomas – a wicked man who was often drunk.

JOSIE: Like all your friends.

DIANA / RUBY: Be quiet / shut up Josie! (etc)

ANNE: One night, as he was walking home from a public house, he was pursued by a headless – lamb – of fire. At once he knew – it was the spirit of his brother, and he would surely die within nine days.

Pause.

JOSIE: So did he?

RUBY: Did he, Anne?

ANNE: No… But he died two years afterwards. So you see… *it was really true.*

JOSIE: That was in Nova Scotia. Things like that don't happen here.

ANNE: You mean you don't know about – *the haunted wood?*

JOSIE: There's no such thing.

DIANA: Oh, isn't there?

JOSIE: Where is it then?

ANNE: It's the spruce grove up over the brook.

DIANA: (*Helpful.*) You know – on your way home, Josie.

JOSIE: Then you're lying. I've walked through that wood a hundred times and never seen one ghost.

ANNE: Ah – but have you ever walked through it *after dark*? When twilight falls – that is when ghosts walk.

JOSIE: What ghosts?

RUBY: A headless highwayman rides up and down the path. And there's all skellingtons behind the trees.

DIANA: Don't forget the White Lady. She walks along the brook, wringing her hands and uttering wails. She appears to foretell a death in the family.

JOSIE: What family?

DIANA: Any family.

Spooky lighting change.

ANNE: But the worst ghost of all – is the little murdered orphan boy. He had epilepsy, and his wicked aunt gave out he died in a fit. But in fact, she beat him to death, just to get her hands on the miserable pittance his mother had left him. And now, his ghost haunts the spruce grove, grovelling on the ground, just as he did in life, and when he sees you he lays his cold, cold fingers on your neck –

GILBERT enters in time to hear the end of ANNE's speech.

GILBERT: Like this!

The normal "school" lighting state slams in. GILBERT touches JOSIE on the back of the neck. JOSIE shrieks, leaps up and runs away. DIANA and RUBY fall about laughing.

RUBY: (*Flirtatious.*) Oh Gilbert Blythe, you'll be the death of me!

DIANA: You must admit Anne, that was pretty funny.

ANNE: I call it cruel. Scaring Josie like that!

The school bell rings. MISS STACY enters, followed by a sulky JOSIE.

MISS STACY: This afternoon, I would like to hold a special class for those students who wish to try for Queen's College. Which of you plan to sit the entrance exam?

GILBERT gestures his assent.

Gilbert – of course. Charlie Sloane? Ruby Gillis?

RUBY: Well, I'll take my teacher's license, but I'll only teach for two years. Then, *of course*, I'll get married.

MISS STACY: Let's just think about the entrance exam for now, shall we? Anne?

ANNE: Oh, I'd love to go to Queen's and pass for a teacher! It's the dream of my life – well, for the last six months anyway.

MISS STACY: I'll add your name to my list, then. (*Doubtful.*) Josie?

JOSIE: Oh, I'm going to Queen's.

MISS STACY: Are you sure, Josie? You'll need to study…

JOSIE: *My father* can pay for me to stay on until I pass. It's not as if *I'm* living on charity.

MISS STACY: Thank you Josie. Diana? No – very well. Jane Andrews…

MISS STACY moves on. ANNE talks aside to DIANA.

ANNE: Diana – why?

DIANA: Mother doesn't think girls need education.

MISS STACY: So, if my Queen's scholars can stay behind – the rest of you may go.

ANNE looks sadly on as DIANA walks out. Music.

Green Gables – Kitchen

ANNE, MATTHEW, MARILLA.

ANNE: Diana's not trying for Queen's, Marilla. Isn't that tragical? I never dreamed we would be parted again – so soon.

MARILLA: Well, you won't be if you fail the entrance exam.

ANNE: I'm sure that *should* be a comfort… But it would be such a disgrace to fail, especially if Gil – if the others passed…

MARILLA: You've been working hard enough. You should pass.

MATTHEW: She'll beat the whole Island.

ANNE: I won't, Matthew, but it's nice of you to think so. Now, I must go and study, or geometry will be my downfall.

ANNE goes out. MATTHEW turns to MARILLA.

MATTHEW: Did you ever notice – does Anne look different from the other girls?

MARILLA: With hair that red, I should say so.

MATTHEW: It's not her looks. It's her dresses. Something about the, er, the, er – (*Mimes.*)

MARILLA: (*Sharply.*) Sleeves?

MATTHEW: Well now, that's it.

MARILLA: She's been hankering after those ridiculous puffed sleeves since she came here. But I'm not wasting my time and money on pampering her vanity.

MATTHEW: Well now… maybe… I could?

MARILLA: Matthew Cuthbert!

MATTHEW: She's been studying so hard. She deserves a present.

MARILLA: I can't stop you. But I'd like to see the day *you* walk into Lawson's store and ask for a girl's dress with puffed sleeves.

MARILLA bustles off, but pauses for one last sharp comment.

Now, *that* would be a present in itself.

MARILLA leaves.

The Riverside

ANNE, RUBY and DIANA. They have a book, oars, a gaudy golden cloth and a lily.

DIANA: Do you think it's right to imagine things like this? Miss Stacy was so cross when Josie told her about the Haunted Wood.

ANNE: *Lancelot and Elaine*'s completely different. (*Brandishing the book.*) It's on the national curriculum.

RUBY: But Mrs Lynde says, play-acting is abominably wicked.

ANNE: This is the olden days of yore. Mrs Lynde isn't even born yet. Besides, it will help to take our minds off the Queen's exams.

RUBY: It's all right for you, Anne – you're sure to pass.

ANNE: I don't think so. I've got a creepy, crawly feeling that I've failed geometry –

RUBY: (*Groans.*) But I failed *everything*, I just know it. Oh well, I suppose I'll just have to get married right away.

DIANA: Well, you won't know anything until the pass list is out, anyway.

ANNE: Fancy living a fortnight in such suspense!

RUBY: Oh, let's not think about it!

ANNE: Very well. Now, where were we…? Elaine has given orders that her lifeless body be covered in cloth of gold and placed on a barge, there to drift down to Camelot, where Sir Lancelot awaits…

RUBY: Who's going to be Elaine?

DIANA: (*Firmly.*) Anne.

ANNE: We can't have an Elaine with red hair. It's so unromantic.

DIANA: But you'll be the most romantically dead. You know you will.

ANNE: Very well.

ANNE ties the cloth around herself.

(*Recites.*) So –
– let there be prepared a chariot-bier
To take me to the river, and a barge
Be ready on the river, clothed in black –

RUBY: (*Interrupts.*) Get in the boat, then, and we'll float you down the river.

ANNE: Ruby, you be King Arthur, and Diana, you be Lancelot – you'd better sort out the rest of the parts yourselves, seeing as I'm dead.

ANNE lies back. RUBY places the lily in her hands.

RUBY: Oh, she does look really dead!

DIANA: What do we do now, Anne?

ANNE sits up, exasperated.

ANNE: Kiss my quiet brows!

DIANA: Oh yes, of course – (*Kisses ANNE.*) Sister, farewell for ever.

RUBY: Farewell, sweet sister.

ANNE: (*With her eyes shut.*) Good, now push me off and meet me at the bridge.

The girls push the boat off.

RUBY: (*Enjoying the drama.*) To the bridge!

The girls run off, taking the book and oars with them.

KATIE: Then something happened that was not at all romantic. The boat began to leak.

ANNE: Dear God – I am afraid I haven't prayed to you as much as I might. Perhaps because Mrs Lynde once told me that you made my hair red *on purpose*, and I haven't cared for you since. However, as you may have noticed, I find myself in a somewhat precarious position…

RUBY and DIANA are standing on desks ("the bridge"). They shout:

DIANA: The boat's leaking!

RUBY screams.

ANNE: We haven't much time, God, so I'll be brief. Excuse me for not closing my eyes, which I know you prefer, but I really need them open, so if you could just see your way to taking me over to one of the bridge-piles, I'll do the rest.

The other actors run on and pile chairs and desks around ANNE. She jumps up and clings to them.

KATIE: The flat drifted under the bridge and then promptly sank in midstream.

RUBY: Row, Anne! Row for your life!

DIANA: (*Brandishing the oars.*) She can't!

> *DIANA and RUBY scream.*

> Where is she?

ANNE: I'm here!

RUBY: (*Hysterical.*) Oh, she's dead, she's dead!

ANNE: Girls, I'm here!

DIANA: She isn't! We'll find her. Come *on*!

> *They run off, leaving ANNE clinging to the bottom of the bridge.*

ANNE: Girls…

KATIE: Anne looked at the depths beneath her, wavering with long, oily shadows. And just as she thought she could hold on no longer, Gilbert Blythe came rowing under the bridge…

> *GILBERT appears from behind the bridge-pile.*

GILBERT: Anne Shirley!

ANNE: Mr Blythe. Might you offer me some assistance?

KATIE: There was no help for it. Anne scrambled down into Gilbert's rowing boat.

GILBERT: How on earth did you get there?

ANNE: We were – studying *Lancelot and Elaine.*

GILBERT: In depth, I see. Is this your coverlet of cloth of gold?

> *ANNE pulls off the cloth.*

> Elaine the fair, Elaine the loveable –

ANNE: Stop.

GILBERT: Elaine the Lily Maid of Astolat…

ANNE: Stop it.

GILBERT: Who was playing Sir Lancelot?

ANNE: Mr Blythe! Would you please take me to the landing?

KATIE: Gilbert obligingly rowed to the landing and Anne, disdaining assistance, sprang nimbly on shore.

ANNE: I'm very much obliged to you.

She turns to go.

GILBERT: Anne, wait!

ANNE: Mr Blythe?

GILBERT: I'm sorry I said your – you know – was like – you know what. But it was so long ago, Anne! Can't we be friends? We'll be going to Queen's soon.

ANNE: If I pass.

GILBERT: Of course you'll pass! Come on, Anne! Are you going to ignore me for the whole year in Charlottetown?

ANNE: I suppose that *might* be difficult…

GILBERT: I knew you'd see sense. I can't believe you held a grudge so long about that silly joke.

ANNE: (*Freezing again.*) *Carrots?* Is that what you call a *joke?*

GILBERT: It was! I *like* your hair!

ANNE looks at GILBERT – is this a compliment?

Even if it *is* red…

ANNE slaps GILBERT with a force that surprises both of them.

I never learn, do I?

ANNE: No. My answer is no. I shall never be friends with you, Gilbert Blythe. Please do not ask me again.

ANNE storms off. GILBERT shouts after her:

GILBERT: You got your wish, Anne Shirley.

Green Gables – A few hours later

MATTHEW is smoking his pipe. MARILLA enters.

MARILLA: (*To MATTHEW.*) Where's Anne?

MATTHEW: Well now, I – guess she's up in her room.

MARILLA: You haven't seen her?

MATTHEW: Not since breakfast.

MARILLA, concerned, shouts upstairs.

MARILLA: Anne ! Anne!

ANNE: (*Off-stage, pathetic.*) What is it, Marilla?

MARILLA: (*To herself.*) Thank the Lord.

MATTHEW: Why Marilla, what is it?

MARILLA composes herself and is stern again.

MARILLA: (*Shouting up.*) Anne Shirley, I've been hearing all sorts of things about you!

MATTHEW: (*To MARILLA.*) What's happened?

MARILLA: (*To MATTHEW.*) I wish I knew! There's gossip all over the village. Ruby and Diana say she's drowned, and Mrs Lynde says she heard that Anne hit Gilbert Blythe – again! (*Calling up.*) Anne, you come down here this minute and explain yourself!

ANNE: (*Off-stage.*) I can't! I can never show my face in public again. Never!

MARILLA: What is it then? (*Pause.*) Are you sick?

ANNE: (*Off-stage.*) No. But please, don't make me come down, and don't look at me. My career is closed. I'm in the depths of despair. I don't even care if I get into Queen's now. Little things like that are of no importance because I won't be able to go anywhere, ever again.

MATTHEW and MARILLA look at each other.

MARILLA: Anne Shirley, come in here *this minute* and tell me what's going on.

Slowly, ANNE walks in. Her hair is streaked with green. MARILLA takes a deep breath and keeps calm.

Anne. What happened to your hair?

ANNE: I dyed it.

MARILLA: Well, you might have dyed it a decent colour.

ANNE: I didn't mean to dye it green! The pedlar said it would turn my hair a beautiful raven black.

MARILLA: Did he now?

ANNE: He was a German Jew, trying to raise money to bring his wife and children over to Canada. He spoke so feelingly that it touched my heart – I had to help in such a worthy object.

MARILLA: Well, I hope you've got your eyes opened now. Do you see where your vanity has led you?

ANNE: (*Sobbing.*) Yes, to green hair!

MARILLA: Goodness knows what's to be done. I suppose the first thing is to give it a good wash.

ANNE: I've been scrubbing it for hours!

MARILLA: Well, if the dye won't come out I'll have to cut it out.

ANNE: (*Horrified.*) Cut it out!

MARILLA: Or you could just leave it green…

ANNE: You're right. (*Dismal.*) I will have to cut off my hair.

MATTHEW: (*Trying to help.*) There now, it ain't so bad, is it?

ANNE: My heart is broken. Girls in books lose their hair in fevers or sell it to get money for some good deed. But this isn't even romantic. I fear it is the end of everything…

MARILLA: Well, I never thought you were vain about your hair, of all things!

ANNE: Nor did I; however, it seems that I was. But it is too late – my fate is sealed, alas. (*She fumbles in her apron pocket for her scissors, and presents them to MARILLA dramatically.*) Please cut it off at once, Marilla, and have it over with.

MARILLA takes the scissors.

MARILLA: You'll have to come over by the kitchen window then, I can't see by this light.

ANNE: (*As she goes.*) I'll do penance every time I pass a mirror, and see how ugly I am… Josie Pye once told me that I looked a perfect scarecrow, and now I fear that she will be right…

ANNE walks off, followed by MARILLA.

MATTHEW: (*To himself.*) What was it?… Puffed sleeves…

Music.

Lawson's General Store

A sign – "General Store". MATTHEW stands, waiting.

MATTHEW: Puffed sleeves… Puffed sleeves…

He steps forward, boldly.
FX – Shop bell.

I want to buy some p... puh... some puh...

The source of his fear is MISS HARRIS, voluptuous shop assistant.

MISS HARRIS: Can I help you, Mr Cuthbert?

MATTHEW: (*Panicking.*) Where's Mr Lawson?

MISS HARRIS: He left me in charge – I'm his niece. So what can I do for you this evening, Mr Cuthbert?

MATTHEW: Have you got any... any hayseed?

MISS HARRIS: We only keep hayseed in the spring, Mr Cuthbert.

MATTHEW: (*Making a huge effort.*) Well now, in that case I'd like to see a... a garden rake.

MISS HARRIS: I'm afraid we're out of stock, Mr Cuthbert. Will there be anything else, Mr Cuthbert?

MATTHEW: It's not too much trouble... Can I take a look at... I might as well see some...

MISS HARRIS: Yes, Mr Cuthbert?

MATTHEW: Sugar.

MISS HARRIS: We've only got brown, Mr Cuthbert.

MATTHEW: I'll take twenty pounds.

MISS HARRIS: Right you are, Mr Cuthbert.

MISS HARRIS gives MATTHEW an enormous bag of sugar. The shop bell rings as MATTHEW backs away. MISS HARRIS exits.

Outside Lawson's General Store

MATTHEW bumps into RACHEL LYNDE. He looks sheepish and tries to hide his bag of sugar.

MRS LYNDE: Matthew Cuthbert! You look as if you've seen a ghost!

MATTHEW: Do you want some sugar?

MRS LYNDE: Not if it's that coarse, brown stuff I don't.

MATTHEW: Mrs Lynde – Rachel – you know about – women's – things, don't you?

MRS LYNDE: Is this something to do with Anne?

MATTHEW: Her dresses. The other girls – the sleeves – they make 'em different. I wanted to get her a – with – you know – the – could you – see your way to –

MRS LYNDE: Making up a dress for Anne? With puffed sleeves?

MATTHEW nods, thankfully.

I'm so glad you asked me that! The way Marilla dresses her is a shame, that's what. But to think of you taking notice! Matthew Cuthbert, it's as if you've been asleep for the last sixty years, and you've suddenly woken up!

MATTHEW: Well now – I – I guess it is.

Music.

Green Gables – Later

MARILLA and MATTHEW.

MARILLA: (*To MATTHEW.*) So this is what you've been grinning about to yourself for two weeks? I knew you were up to some foolishness. I must say, I didn't think Anne needed any new dresses. And as for those sleeves – I could make two good petticoats out of them! She'll have to go through the door sideways! (*Sighs.*) Well, let's see you then, child.

ANNE enters, with short hair, wearing a lovely dress with puffed sleeves.

Hmm! Well, aren't you even going to thank Matthew?

MATTHEW: What's wrong, Anne? Don't you like it?

ANNE: It's perfectly exquisite. Matthew, words can't express my thankfulness. The sleeves…

MARILLA: It's a sinful waste but now you've got it, see you take care of it. Put your apron over it for breakfast.

ANNE: Breakfast seems so commonplace at a moment like this…

DIANA runs in, with a newspaper.

DIANA: Anne! Anne!

ANNE: The pass list? Did we…

DIANA shows ANNE the paper.

DIANA: Anne, you've passed – passed the very first in the whole of PE Island!

ANNE: (*Reading.*) Me and Gilbert both… we're ties.

DIANA: But your name is first. First out of two hundred!

DIANA hugs ANNE. MATTHEW and MARILLA grab for the paper and read it.

Father just brought the paper home from Bright River – it won't be here till tomorrow by mail. When I saw the list I just rushed over like a wild thing!

ANNE: Did Ruby –

DIANA: Oh, she passed. Even Josie Pye scraped through. How can you be so calm, Anne? If it were me I'd just go crazy with joy!

ANNE: I'm just dazzled inside, I… I never dreamed of this.

MATTHEW: (*Calm.*) Well now, I knew you'd beat them all easy.

ANNE runs to MATTHEW and hugs him. MARILLA feels slightly left out.

DIANA: You won't find a new best friend in Charlottetown, will you?

ANNE: Never!

ANNE hugs DIANA. MARILLA feels more left out.

MARILLA: (*To DIANA.*) Anne's done pretty well, I must say. (*To ANNE.*) You'll have to keep up your hard work at Queen's, mind.

ANNE: Of course I will! I intend to take my First Class teacher's licence in one year – that way I can start teaching and earning when I'm sixteen.

MARILLA: You've got it all planned out, I see. Well, I suppose you'll want to tell your friends?

ANNE: Ruby will be so relieved to know she passed too! May I go, Marilla?

MARILLA: Oh yes, you go. Go.

ANNE: Thank you!

ANNE runs out, followed by DIANA. MARILLA brushes away a tear, impatient.

MATTHEW: (*Concerned.*) Are you having trouble with your eyes again, Marilla?

MARILLA: She looks so – different in that dress… and with that hair… So tall, and stylish. As if she didn't belong in Avonlea at all… Which she don't, of course. But still. I just don't know how she got to be so grown up all of a sudden. And now, she's going away to college…

MATTHEW: She'll be able to come home often.

MARILLA: It won't be the same. But there. Men can't understand these things.

MARILLA goes out, followed by MATTHEW.
Music.

Queen's Common Room, Charlottetown

Some time later. ANNE is writing a letter.

ANNE: When I got my place at Queen's I thought all my dreams had come true, but I never thought I'd suffer such an agony of homesickness. Oh Diana, please don't tell Matthew and Marilla how much I miss them. I'm trying to concentrate on my studies – imagine Matthew's face if I won the class Gold Medal! The end of term seems a hundred years away. I miss Avonlea so much, I'm even finding myself glad to see –

JOSIE PYE enters.

Josie Pye!

JOSIE: I am literally starving. Got anything eatable?

ANNE produces some cake from a bag and watches it disappear into JOSIE's mouth.

I guessed Marilla would load you up with cake. You've been crying! I suppose you're homesick? Some people have so little self-control. You shouldn't cry, Anne – your nose and eyes get red, and then you seem *all* red.

RUBY enters.

ANNE: Ruby. Thank goodness.

RUBY: Cake? Well, maybe just a teeny piece.

JOSIE passes RUBY a chunk of cake.

JOSIE: Did you see the French professor...?

JOSIE and RUBY gasp and clutch their chests in an exaggerated manner.

RUBY: What a duck, isn't he? His moustache gives me kerwallops of the heart.

ANNE: That sounds unpleasant.

RUBY: (*Through a mouthful of cake.*) What's wrong with you?

JOSIE: Anne's homesick.

ANNE: Aren't you?

RUBY: Oh, no! Town's too jolly after that poky old Avonlea. I wonder how we existed there for so long!

JOSIE: Did I tell you? Frank Stockley's taking me to the park to hear the band tonight.

RUBY: Oh? Well, *I'm* going with Gilbert Blythe. What about you, Anne?

ANNE: I – think I'll stay home. I want to study.

JOSIE: Yes, I would, if I were you. I hear Matthew and Marilla are terribly in debt. If you fail this year, they won't be able to send you back, you know.

ANNE: I won't fail.

JOSIE: I forgot, you always have to be the best at everything, Queen Anne. (*Cutting, to RUBY.*) I suppose she thinks she'll win the Avery scholarship.

With a derisive snort, JOSIE leaves.

ANNE: What's the Avery Scholarship?

RUBY: I don't know. Gilbert –

ANNE: No!

It's too late. GILBERT BLYTHE comes over.

RUBY: Gilbert, Anne wants to know about the – the –

ANNE: (*Embarrassed.*) Avery Scholarship.

RUBY: (*Beaming.*) Yes, that thing.

GILBERT: The Avery Scholarship. A prize for the best student in English. Two hundred and fifty dollars a year for four years at Redmond College.

ANNE: Thank you, Mr Blythe.

GILBERT: Glad to be of service, Miss Shirley. I er – take it that you ladies will be competing?

ANNE: (*Over-casual.*) Well, it's fun to have ambitions, isn't it, Ruby?

RUBY: It's no fun to be bothering about books and that sort of thing. I can't wait to be married so I won't have to. How about you, Gil?

GILBERT: Oh, I'll give it a shot. I'll need to take my degree if I'm going to train as a doctor.

ANNE: (*Surprised.*) You – a doctor, Mr Blythe?

RUBY: Why on earth would you want to be around sick people?

GILBERT: Somebody once defined man as a fighting animal. You have to fight something all through life. I want to fight disease and pain and ignorance. After all, they're all part of one another.

RUBY: I don't understand half the things you say, Gilbert Blythe!

GILBERT: That's why I like you.

GILBERT blows a mock kiss to RUBY and walks off.

RUBY: That Gilbert! Sometimes he talks as funny as you do, Anne.

ANNE: You're spending a lot of time with him, aren't you?

RUBY: Well, he's mad about me of course, but he's not the only one. I've got ever so many men on the string, and they're *all* crazy for me.

ANNE: You can't find just one in his right mind?

RUBY: Frank Stockley's got so much more *dash* about him, but Gilbert's so much handsomer. Which would you choose, Anne, if you were me?

ANNE: I wouldn't.

RUBY: Oh, I forgot. You'd probably prefer a good book.

RUBY puts the last of ANNE's cake in her mouth and walks off. ANNE returns to her letter.

ANNE: I don't think I like Ruby Gillis any more.

Music.

Green Gables – Kitchen

Some time later. MATTHEW, MARILLA and MRS LYNDE. MARILLA is poring over a letter from ANNE.

MARILLA: She says she's looking forward to coming home… It doesn't seem possible that the term's nearly over.

MATTHEW: (*Quietly.*) Three weeks tomorrow.

MRS LYNDE: What else does she say?

MARILLA: Why don't you read it yourself?

MARILLA hands MRS LYNDE the letter.

MRS LYNDE: (*Taking the letter.*) Are your eyes still bothering you?

MARILLA: Worse and worse. I can't read or sew with any comfort now. The doctor says I need to see an oculist and I guess I'll have to.

MRS LYNDE: (*Reading.*) Anne thinks she's done pretty well in her exams.

MARILLA: Well let's hope she's passed at any rate, for we can't afford to send her back. We've precious little to spare at the moment.

MRS LYNDE: Who has? By the way, I've been hearing talk about the Abbey Bank. They say it's real shaky. Thomas and I have moved all our money to the Savings Bank and if you take my advice, Marilla, you'll do the same.

MATTHEW: Well now… We've always banked at the Abbey.

MRS LYNDE: Then you shouldn't any more.

MATTHEW: We're too old to change our ways now.

MATTHEW gets up and goes out.

MARILLA: (*Apologetically.*) Old Mr Abbey was a great friend of Father's, you see.

MRS LYNDE: Marilla, is Matthew quite well?

MARILLA: No, he isn't. He's had some real bad spells with his heart this spring. Maybe he'll pick up when Anne comes home.

MRS LYNDE: He's seemed older-like, ever since she went away.

MARILLA: Haven't we all?

Music.

Queen's Common Room

ANNE paces, tense. If possible, her hair is long again, possibly up, she looks older. RUBY strolls in.

RUBY: Say, Anne! Ain't you heard? The results are out!

ANNE groans.

Are you coming to look at the bulletin board?

ANNE: I can't do it, Ruby. I haven't the moral courage.

RUBY: You'll have to face it some time.

ANNE: No. You must read it, and come and tell me. If I have failed just say so, and whatever you do, *don't* sympathise with me.

RUBY: To hear you go on, anyone would think those old exams were actually important!

JOSIE runs in.

JOSIE: Anne! Anne! Have you heard?

ANNE: Heard what?

A cheer outside.

JOSIE: Gilbert Blythe's won the gold medal! Well, I guess that *proves* he's the best scholar! Aren't you coming to congratulate him?

ANNE: Naturally.

GILBERT enters (with other scholars if possible). RUBY and JOSIE run to him.

RUBY: Hurrah for Gilbert Blythe, Gold medalist! Hip hip –

ALL SCHOLARS: Hooray!

ANNE: Congratulations, Mr Blythe.

ANNE offers GILBERT her hand. He shakes it.

GILBERT: Thank you. You didn't do so badly yourself.

ANNE: Please, don't patronise me.

GILBERT: I wasn't, I thought – didn't you *want* to win the Avery?

ANNE: *What?*

GILBERT: You didn't know?

ANNE: I was just – I was going to… I was…

ANNE swallows.

GILBERT: Hurrah for Miss Anne Shirley, winner of the Avery Scholarship! Hip hip –

ALL SCHOLARS: Hooray!

The Avonlea gang take it in turns to hug and congratulate ANNE.

RUBY: Oh Anne, I'm so proud!

ANNE: I can't take it in… I feel as if someone had handed me the moon and I didn't know what to do with it.

JOSIE: So, all that work paid off, Anne. Well, I'm glad they chose you. You're sure to pass your BA.

ANNE: (*Surprised and touched.*) Thank you, Josie.

JOSIE: Most girls would throw it all away to get married, you see. I guess that's why they chose you. Because of your hair.

It's GILBERT's turn. His easy smile disarms ANNE, but she is still afraid he is mocking her.

GILBERT: Anne. What can I say?

ANNE: I don't know. I… I must write home – right away!

ANNE rushes off.

GILBERT: Anne –

JOSIE: Redheads! So temperamental.

RUBY: (*Flirtatious.*) Well, Gilbert Blythe. What shall we do to celebrate?

GILBERT leaves with RUBY. JOSIE (and other scholars) follow behind.

The Classroom

KATIE approaches MARIAN, timidly.

KATIE: Excuse me?

MARIAN: What do you want?

KATIE: I want to know… How is Mr Carr?

MARIAN: Not doing so well, I heard.

KATIE: Oh. When is he coming back?

MARIAN: I don't know if he will. When you get a stroke at his time of life…

KATIE: Yes.

MARIAN: Well, there you are. Life isn't like in your books, you know. It's not all fairy tales and happy endings.

MARIAN goes.

KATIE: (*Quietly.*) Why do you think you need to tell me that?

JOSIE and RUBY enter.

JOSIE: Look, there it is. Might have known we'd find it here.

RUBY: Missing your boyfriend are you, hippy?

KATIE: Please, just leave me alone!

JOSIE: Gonna make me?

MARIAN re-enters.

MARIAN: No, I am. Go on, move it! (*Brandishes her mop.*)

JOSIE: If you touch me, my dad'll –

MARIAN: Yes, I'd like a word with your dad. We'll have a little chat with my Judy down the off-licence. I think he'll be surprised to find how many alcopops and fags your pocket money will stretch to these days. But I tell you what. If I don't see your ugly face hanging around here, there'll be nothing to remind me to talk to him. Will there?

Pause. JOSIE is thwarted.

I'm going to count to ten. One – two –

RUBY: C'mon, let's split.

JOSIE: Whatever.

JOSIE and RUBY leave.

MARIAN: I were going to visit Mr Carr tonight. Thought he might appreciate a new face, for a change. If you're not too busy.

KATIE: No – I'm not.

MARIAN: Well come on. I haven't got all day.

KATIE: Of course.

MARIAN goes to exit and pauses.

MARIAN: You might want to bring that book of yours.

MARIAN exits, followed by KATIE.
Music.

Bright River Station

KATIE and ANNE mirror their original positions in the first Bright River scene in Act One. ANNE has a case. MATTHEW meets ANNE.

MATTHEW: Well now, Anne.

ANNE: Matthew!

ANNE runs to him. MATTHEW picks up ANNE's bag with effort. ANNE takes it from him.

Let me.

MATTHEW: Seems I'm growing old, Anne. I keep forgetting.

ANNE: You've been working too hard. Why won't you take things easier?

MATTHEW: Habit, I guess.

ANNE: I wish I'd been the boy you sent for – I could have helped you with the farm.

MATTHEW: Well now, I'd rather have you than a dozen boys, Anne. Just mind you that. It wasn't a boy that took the Avery scholarship now, was it? It was a girl – my girl – my girl that I'm proud of.

ANNE hugs MATTHEW.

We'd best get on now, Anne. They're all waiting for you at Green Gables.

ANNE: Then let's go home.

They exit together.
KATIE watches them go.

Green Gables – Later

Applause from DIANA, MRS BARRY and MRS LYNDE. ANNE enters, followed by MATTHEW. She flies into DIANA's arms.

DIANA: Anne!

ANNE: Oh, it's so good to be back!

MATTHEW: (*To MARILLA.*) Reckon you're glad we kept her?

MARILLA: It's not the first time I've been glad, Matthew Cuthbert. (*She hands him some letters.*) And the Lord knows we've precious little else to be glad of right now. If these aren't more wretched bills I'll be surprised.

MATTHEW goes aside to read the post as ANNE rushes up to MARILLA.

ANNE: Oh Marilla, you can't think how I've missed Green Gables. And you. All of you.

MRS LYNDE: You're a credit to your friends, Anne Shirley, that's what.

MRS BARRY: I suppose you won't be teaching now, Anne?

ANNE: No, I'm going to Redmond in September. Isn't it wonderful? To think – me, a BA!

MRS LYNDE: Pride goes before a fall.

ANNE: I'm not proud. Just – thankful. For everything.

MATTHEW's letter slips from his grasp.

MARILLA: Matthew?

ANNE: Matthew – what's the matter? Are you sick?

ANNE, MARILLA and MRS LYNDE crowd round MATTHEW.

MRS LYNDE: He's out cold.

MARILLA: His heart trouble…

MRS BARRY: Diana, run and fetch the doctor. Quick as you can.

DIANA speeds off.

MARILLA: (*Distraught.*) Matthew, wake up! Matthew!

MRS LYNDE: Most likely some sudden shock that's done it.

MRS LYNDE looks suspiciously at the letter in MATTHEW's hand. She reads it, as ANNE and MARILLA try to revive MATTHEW.

MARILLA: I've been real worried about him all year – told him to go easier, but he wouldn't spare himself... Would you, Matthew?

MRS LYNDE: (*Gently.*) Oh, Marilla... The Abbey Bank's failed. All your savings...

MARILLA: It's only money, after all. What does it matter?

ANNE: It doesn't matter, Matthew.

MRS LYNDE takes MATTHEW's pulse and puts her ear over his heart. She glances over to MRS BARRY.

MRS BARRY: Marilla – dear –

MARILLA: No – no!

MRS LYNDE: I'm so sorry.

MARILLA collapses into grief. MRS BARRY tries to comfort her.

ANNE: You don't – you can't think –

MRS LYNDE: Child... Look at him. (*ANNE looks at MATTHEW.*) When you've seen that look as often as I have you'll know what it means.

Fade to black.

SONG: "Wayfaring Stranger" (Reprise)

FULL COMPANY:
> *I know dark clouds will gather round me*
> *I know my way is rough and steep.*
> *But beauteous fields lie just beyond me*
> *Where souls redeemed their vigil keep.*
> *I'm going there to meet my Saviour*
> *To sing his praise forever more*
> *I'm only going over Jordan*
> *I'm only going over home.*

The Churchyard

ANNE and MARILLA hold flowers.

ANNE: (*Calm, with deep feeling.*) Matthew, I know you love the white Scotch roses best. I'm going to plant a rose tree so that you're surrounded by them always. It seems a terrible thing, Matthew, but I can't cry for you, even though I love you so much and you were so kind to me. I stand at my window and pray – I look to the stars beyond the hills – and I can't find you – and still the tears won't come. All I feel is this dull – dry – ache. But I can see you – I can hear you – and as long as I live I'll never forget what you called me. "My girl, that I'm proud of."

MARILLA feels it's her turn, but eulogising doesn't come easy to her.

MARILLA: You were always a good – kind – brother – to me.

ANNE and MARILLA bend and put down their offerings. GILBERT enters, sees them and approaches, hesitantly.

ANNE: (*Surprised.*) Gilbert Blythe!

GILBERT: Anne – I – I don't want to intrude. I just wanted to say, I – (*To MARILLA.*) Miss Cuthbert, if you need any help – next year, when Anne's away –

MARILLA: But won't you be going to Redmond College, too?

GILBERT: No. I mean, I hope to, eventually, but I need to save for my tuition.

MARILLA: How will you do that?

GILBERT: By teaching at Avonlea school. Miss Stacy's leaving, and the trustees have kindly offered me the position…

ANNE: (*Surprised.*) You're not going to Redmond, Mr Blythe?

As ANNE and GILBERT talk, MARILLA quietly withdraws.

GILBERT: No. You got your wish, Anne. You're finally rid of me. You'll be the first BA from Avonlea. Congratulations.

ANNE: Thank you.

GILBERT: You deserve it. If anyone does. I – I've never met anyone like you.

ANNE: Mr Blythe –

GILBERT: Don't. Just don't. I knew from the moment I met you that I never stood a chance.

GILBERT leaves. ANNE is isolated on the darkened stage. Church bells, then – silence.
We hear MARILLA crying.

ANNE: Marilla! – Marilla?

Green Gables – Kitchen

MARILLA sits at the table, weeping as if she has given up hope.

ANNE: Marilla. Oh, Marilla.

ANNE comforts MARILLA. MARILLA tries to control herself.

MARILLA: (*Of herself.*) It's wicked to cry so. It can't bring him back.

ANNE: I know – I know.

ANNE cries, too. MARILLA puts her arm around her to comfort her.

MARILLA: There – there – don't you cry, dearie. God knows best, after all.

ANNE: (*Shakes her head.*) The tears don't hurt me like that ache did. Let me cry for him now. Oh Marilla, what will we do without him?

MARILLA: We've got each other, Anne.

ANNE: Yes…

MARILLA: I want to tell you now, when I can.

ANNE: What?

MARILLA: I've never found it easy to – talk – from my heart. Not like you. But – Anne, I've been kind of harsh with you, but you mustn't think – it was only Matthew that loved you.

ANNE: I never did.

MARILLA: The truth is – you're like my own flesh and blood, and – well, I don't know how I lived before you came to Green Gables. That's all.

ANNE hugs MARILLA. A moment as they comfort each other.

ANNE: I will be, still. Always. I'm going to take good care of you, Marilla. You seem so tired –

MARILLA: It's not just – well, you might as well know, Anne – I saw that oculist yesterday.

ANNE: What did he say?

MARILLA: If I go on as I am, I'll be blind in six months.

ANNE: But you won't! I mean, he can save your sight – can't he?

MARILLA: He says I *may* not get any worse –

ANNE: Well then!

MARILLA: If I wear the glasses he's given me –

ANNE: Yes.

MARILLA: And if I give up all sewing and reading –

ANNE: Marilla –

MARILLA: Oh, yes. And if I'm careful not to cry.

She laughs bitterly. ANNE has never seen MARILLA like this.

ANNE: (*Slowly.*) You know, Marilla –

MARILLA: (*Interrupting.*) But there's no good talking about it. If you'll get me a cup of tea I'll be thankful.

ANNE goes as if to make tea, just as MRS LYNDE enters.

MRS LYNDE enters.

MRS LYNDE: Marilla, Thomas wanted to speak to you about (*Sees ANNE.*) – that business matter.

ANNE: What? What is it?

MARILLA: She'll have to know soon, anyway. (*To ANNE.*) Mr Lynde is going to buy Green Gables.

ANNE: You can't sell Green Gables.

MARILLA: I don't know what else is to be done. Every cent of our money went in that bank! If my eyes were strong I could manage, with a hired man to run the farm, but I can't stay here alone.

ANNE: You won't have to. I'm not going to Redmond. I won't take the scholarship.

MARILLA: Now, Anne –

ANNE: How could I, after all you've done for me? Mr Lynde can *rent* the farm next year – (*To MRS LYNDE.*) he'll do that, won't he?

MRS LYNDE: I daresay he can be persuaded.

ANNE: And I shall teach. I know Gilbert's to have the Avonlea school, but the White Sands school is available, and Miss Stacy will give me a good reference.

MARILLA: Rachel, talk some sense into her.

MRS LYNDE: She's talking sense already.

MARILLA: I won't let you sacrifice yourself for me.

ANNE: There is no sacrifice. Not as long as we can keep Green Gables.

MARILLA: I'll make it up to you, Anne.

ANNE: You already have. More than you could ever know.

MARILLA: You blessed girl... (*Gives up.*) Well, Diana Barry will be pleased, anyhow.

ANNE: You're right! I must run over and tell her.

MARILLA: Anne...

ANNE: Don't worry – I'll be back in time to fix supper.

ANNE dashes out.

MRS LYNDE: Ain't you proud of that Anne-girl? I am.

MARILLA wipes away a tear.

Marilla?

MARILLA: (*Rising.*) I'll just see about that cup of tea.

Music.

The Haunted Wood

Some hours later. Sunset. DIANA and ANNE walking and talking.

DIANA: I don't want to lose you, but I never thought you'd give up your ambitions.

ANNE: I'm more ambitious than ever! When I left Queen's my future seemed to stretch right out before me for many miles. Now there's a bend in the road. I wonder what lies beyond it…

DIANA: Well, I'm glad you'll be here for another year, at least.

The girls embrace and part. As DIANA goes, she encounters GILBERT.

GILBERT: Diana.

DIANA: Gilbert.

With a quick glance at ANNE, DIANA runs off. GILBERT nods courteously to ANNE but moves on.

ANNE: Don't go.

GILBERT stops, looks at ANNE inquiringly.

Mr Blythe, I want to call a truce. You see, the thing is – I'm not going to Redmond. I'm going to stay here and teach. And it seems to me – since I'll only be at White Sands – that we may as well – You know?

GILBERT: No. I don't know.

ANNE: Then there is nothing more to say.

GILBERT: I don't know about White Sands. I guess you're going to teach right here in Avonlea. The trustees have decided to give you the school.

ANNE: But they'd promised it to you!

GILBERT: Well, they didn't know any better, at the time. But when Mrs Lynde kindly informed me that *the Avery winner* wanted the school, I felt it was only fair to withdraw my application. Don't look at me like that! I've taken the post at White Sands School, so you'll have to teach in Avonlea. You belong here, after all.

ANNE: Gilbert…

ANNE holds out her hand to GILBERT. He looks at it.

GILBERT: What does this mean? Can you possibly have forgiven me?

ANNE: I think I forgave you a long time ago.

GILBERT takes ANNE's hand.

GILBERT: I knew it! We were meant to be good friends.

ANNE: Well, we've been good enemies. We even quarrelled when you saved my life!

GILBERT: "The lily maid of Astolat
Lay smiling, like a star in blackest night,
And smacked Sir Lancelot about his face."

ANNE: Stop! What a stubborn little goose I was!

GILBERT: Well, I did call you "Carrots", didn't I?

ANNE: "Never yet
Was noble man but made ignoble talk.
He makes no friend who never made a foe."

ANNE holds out her hand to GILBERT. He takes it.

GILBERT: "Are ye so wise? Ye were not once so wise."

ANNE shivers and pulls her hand away.

ANNE: This wood is *really* haunted now, by old memories.

GILBERT: Haunted?

ANNE: We've got years of lost conversations to catch up on.

GILBERT: Or we could look to the future.

ANNE: Yes… The skies seem to have closed in somewhat since I came home. But I still have Green Gables, and my imagination – and I've got Marilla, and Diana, and…

GILBERT: And?

ANNE: And… you never know what is around the bend in the road.

ANNE smiles at GILBERT as they walk off together.

KATIE: They walked together down the long hill that sloped to the Lake of Shining Waters. Home lights twinkled among the trees, and beyond lay the sea, misty and purple, with its haunting, unceasing murmur.

The Classroom

KATIE, alone.

KATIE: "God's in his heaven, all's right with the world", whispered Anne.

KATIE closes the book. She looks at ANNE. ANNE looks back at KATIE.

The End